TWELVE MODERN APOSTLES

⌐Twelve Modern Apostles
And Their Creeds

By
GILBERT K. CHESTERTON
BISHOP CHARLES L. SLATTERY
DR. HENRY SLOANE COFFIN
and others

With an Introduction by
THE RT. REV. WILLIAM RALPH INGE

Essay Index Reprint Series

BOOKS FOR LIBRARIES PRESS, INC.
FREEPORT, NEW YORK

First Published 1926
Reprinted 1968

LIBRARY OF CONGRESS CATALOG CARD NUMBER:
68-16982

PRINTED IN THE UNITED STATES OF AMERICA

Foreword

AN enlightening feature of these corner-stones of modern faith—as laid by Bishop Slattery, Episcopalian, Dr. Crothers, Unitarian, Gilbert Chesterton, Catholic, and all the rest—is their tendency, in keeping with these days of spiritual progress, to rise above individual creeds and to stand outside of denominational barriers.

Most unusual in this respect is the vivid and hopeful paper of the Rt. Rev. William Ralph Inge, brilliant Dean of St. Paul's, London. Although written independently of the series, (each of which was written independently of the other), there could be published no more fitting introduction to "The Twelve Modern Apostles and Their Creeds." The future Christianity, according to the Dean of St. Paul's, will not accept the authority either of an infallible institution, or of an infallible book. It will be a religion of the spirit; it will express the religious philosophy of those who are erroneously called "modernists,"—erroneously because their beliefs are as old as Christianity itself. But obviously this true religion will not convert the world at large. Neither is there cause to fear that the light kindled in Galilee will ever be put out.

CONTENTS

TWELVE MODERN APOSTLES

THE FUTURE OF CHRISTIANITY

By

WILLIAM RALPH INGE

Dean of St. Paul's

THE white man must have a religion, and that religion must be Christianity. So Ernst Troeltsch wrote a year before his death, adding that, together with this conviction, his own faith was becoming more radical and super-denominational every year. His attitude, and the course of mental development which led to it, is, I believe, typical of the educated thought of our day. But a short defense of his second statement, that our religion must be Christian, is perhaps desirable, since we sometimes hear it said that we want a new religion. A new religion cannot be had for the asking, any more than a new political and social organization. We might as well try to build a tree. There have been creative periods in religion, but this is not one

[3]

of them, nor does the West seem to be the part of the world where they arise. Religions are exotics in Europe and America; in the East they grow wild, luxuriating sometimes into the strangest fruits and flowers. The West occasionally attempts something new, but in our time it has produced nothing more respectable than Mormonism, Spiritualism, and Christian Science. The great living faiths of the world arose in Asia, and in the millennium which ended with Mohammed.

Christianity has been fortunate as the religion of the dominant races. But though its wide diffusion and political ascendancy may be due to the energy, inventiveness, and perseverance of the European stocks, even an unbeliever might agree with Troeltsch that a religion which has satisfied for so long the most progressive nations of the world must have such spiritual power that it may justly be deemed a revelation of divine truth.

But we must define our terms. What do we mean by Christianity? Historically, Jesus of Nazareth placed himself in the line of the prophetic succession. He was called the prophet of Nazareth in Galilee. His manner of life,—that of a wandering preacher,

—was the way of the Jewish prophets. His message was prophetic,—his stirring call to repentance and amendment, his emphasis on moral conduct, his prediction of a coming "day of the Lord", his disparagement of ritual and tradition, his conflicts with the priests, all belong to the prophetic tradition. His teaching was individual and universal; he had no thought of founding a new religion or a rival hierarchy; though his enemies saw more clearly than his disciples that he was in fact undermining the authority of the Jewish Church. He was no revolutionary; he abolished all barriers by ignoring them. It is impossible to say that the substance of his message was Jewish or Greek, Eastern or Western. It is the pure religion of the Spirit, eternal and world-wide.

The little group of disciples in Palestine who came together again after the tragedy on Mount Calvary were, and wished to be considered, orthodox and pious Jews, who held one distinctive tenet: that the expected Messiah would be their crucified and risen Master. Messianism, however, made only a weak appeal to the Jews of the Dispersion, and was unintelligible to the Gentile world. Under

the influence mainly of St. Paul, the new wine
burst the bottles in which it had been con-
fined; Christianity became a religion for the
Graeco-Roman empire. This was the greatest crisis that the Church has ever encountered. If the Gospel had been purely Semitic
and apocalyptic, as some assert, it could not
have survived such an uprooting. As it was,
Christianity took very kindly to the Greek
language and ways of thinking. Long before
the closing of the New Testament Canon it
had discovered its affinity with the Platonism
of the time, which was drawing into itself
Stoical morality, Pythagorean mysticism, and
all that was most alive in the long tradition of
Greek philosophy. The Orient, it is true, was
lost, and it has never been recovered. Christianity is now perhaps the least Asiatic of all
religions.

The Christianity to which Europe was converted had its roots deep in European civilization. The Catholic Church was the last creative achievement of classical antiquity, which
may be said to have died in giving birth to it.
Its philosophy and theology were mainly
Platonic, its ethics were at first largely Stoical; but the latter were profoundly modified

by the gentler and humbler spirit of the original Gospel, while Judaism contributed certain features which do not fit in well with Platonism. Among these were belief in the creation and end of the world in time, and a stronger hold on divine and human personality. Even more important for the victory of the Church was the Jewish refusal to make any terms with "idolatry", or with the syncretistic mystery cults. Both came back later; but the Church would make no terms with the old religions. Christianity was persecuted as the foe of the old culture, and as an *imperium in imperio*. The fear which inspired the persecutions is intelligible; but they had the natural result of alienating the Church more completely from the classical tradition.

The social and political structure of the old world was crumbling, and the Greeks and Romans were themselves dying out. The city-state was preserved as far as possible under the empire; but civilization was increasingly menaced by the inroads of barbarians from the North and East, and a centralization of a definitely non-European type was forced upon the government. The principate of Augustus had been a camouflaged perpetual dictator-

ship; the monarchy of Diocletian was an undisguised Asiatic sultanate. It was at this
conjuncture that Christianity, after a sharp
struggle, became the official religion of the
Graeco-Roman world.

The great Mediterranean empire soon afterwards split into two halves, of which the
eastern spoke Greek and the western Latin.
The position of the Church was not the same
in the two sections. In the East Roman empire, which lasted till 1453, the form of
government was that known as Caesaropapism. The Church was the right hand of
monarchy, honored and protected by it, but
deprived of independent power. This type of
polity, which is not favorable to the spread of
progressive ideas in Church or State, subsisted
in Russia till the Bolshevik revolution. It is
noteworthy that the Czars were so jealous of
a possible eastern Papacy, that they put the
Patriarchate into commission by constituting
a Holy Synod.

In the West there was no Caesaropapism,
because there was no real Caesar. In the con-
test between the Holy Roman Empire and
the Papacy, the theocracy won. It took to
itself all the attributes of the dead Empire,—

[8]

the boundless prestige of the name of Rome, the claim to universal sovereignty, the autocracy with a graded hierarchy of officials, the praetorian guard of priests and monks, and the right to extinguish by fire and sword any rebellion against the central authority. Like the later Empire, it was a type of government fundamentally alien to the European peoples, but a type which has often shown great strength.

The Dark Ages were a long nightmare of savage anarchy and oppression. At no other time have the gains of civilization been so nearly lost. The dawn came very gradually; the sun rose again at what we call the Renaissance. The city-state once more flourished in Italy, and proved itself again a marvelous forcing-house of genius, though terribly wasteful of its human material. Then the modern European system of sovereign independent states came into being. Henry VIII led the way by proclaiming that "this realm of England is an Empire",—that is, a nation which acknowledges no allegiance to any other Power. The Reformation naturally followed. The pretensions of the priestly Caesar of the Vatican were no more valid than those of the Holy Roman Empire. Thence forward and for ever the twin ideas of a universal Empire and of a universal Church became a reactionary or sentimental dream. Roman Catholicism became sectarian; its claims to a monopoly of divine grace were only a familiar trick of trade.

Modern history has been a record of progressive emancipation. The nations of the West have freed themselves from absolute monarchy, from religious persecution, from oligarchy, and from alien domination. The liberation is now complete, and we may soon be looking for some new integration to save us from dissolution. The further evolution of democracy is quite uncertain. Extremists on both sides are inclined to abandon constitutional political methods. So far, there has been no tendency to revert to theocracy or Caesaropapism, though the Roman Church is only biding its time. It has learned nothing and forgotten nothing.

The Reformation period was in a sense reactionary, inasmuch as the fierce wars of religion checked the humanist movement which accompanied the Renaissance. Humanism was undermining the Catholic Church, but in-

stead of putting in its place a more spiritual
form of religion, it tended to paganism or
pantheism, and was accompanied by moral
license. Northern Europe wanted not this,
but political independence, a reformation of
manners, and a return to the primitive Gospel. This it could not get from Erasmus, still
less from the Italian scholars and artists. But
the wars of religion dragged the Reformation
out of its orbit. They compelled Protestantism, which is essentially a religion of individual inspiration, free inquiry, and ethical strict-
ness, to become a rival religion of authority,
buttressed by the infallible book, as its enemies relied on the infallible Church. It was
disastrous that these struggles followed the
great astronomical discoveries which shat-
tered the mediaeval cosmography. The necessary adjustments were never made; the book
of Genesis foreclosed inquiry no less than the
decrees of the Church. When it was proclaimed that "the Bible is the religion of
Protestants", a large part of the gains of the
Reformation were temporarily lost. An infallible book is at best a poor substitute for an
infallible institution; and when criticism began to do its work on the sacred text, the

foundations of Protestantism gave way. At the present time it shows less vigor, less power of attraction, even less adaptability, than the rival system. It is also naturally fissiparous, and the divisions in the Reformed Churches have long been a scandal.

And yet it is, in my judgment, from Protestantism that we have most to hope. I have said that the Gospel of Christ is the religion of the Spirit in its purest form. In St. Paul's Epistles, in the Epistle to the Hebrews, and in the Fourth Gospel we have a Christian theology and philosophy raised on this foundation, but brought into line with European thought. From that time to the advent of the Dark Ages there was a type of Christian teaching which is sometimes called Platonic, distinguished by its friendly attitude towards secular culture, by its insistence on divine immanence, by its resolute determination to find the seat of authority, not in tradition, or in the arbitrary commands of God, or in an external and supernatural revelation, but in the heart and mind of man, illuminated by the Spirit of Christ. This illumination must be earned, or rather prepared for, by a strenuous course of moral discipline. The religious life begins with faith, which has been defined by Frederick Myers as the resolution to stand or fall by the noblest hypothesis. This venture of the will and conscience progressively verifies itself as we progress on the upward path. That which began as an experiment ends as an experience. We become accustomed to breathe the atmosphere of the spiritual world.

Writers like Clement of Alexandria protest that faith is not an unreasoning acceptance of doctrines imposed by authority. "Faith", he says, "is a compendious knowledge of essentials, while knowledge is a sure and firm demonstration of the things received through faith, carrying us on to unbroken conviction and scientific certainty. There is a first kind of saving change from heathenism to faith, a second from faith to knowledge, and knowledge, as it passes into love, begins at once to establish a mutual friendship between the knower and the known. Perhaps he who has reached this stage is 'equal to the angels'." This kind of teaching will be found in Origen and the Cappadocian Fathers, and even in Augustine. It is the faith of the mediaeval mystics, of the Renaissance on its truly relig-

ious side, and it has been alive continuously
since the Reformation. The little group
called the Cambridge Platonists, in the seventeenth century, exhibits this type of religion
in a singularly pure and attractive form.

We find it again, in the prosaic eighteenth
century, in that robust and eloquent divine,
William Law. It is to-day the faith of Liberal theologians generally, a school which
should repudiate the name of Modernism for
two good reasons. In the first place it is not
modern, but older than Catholicism and much
older than Protestantism. It goes back to the
New Testament, and we may even say to
Christ himself, whose "secret and method", as
Matthew Arnold said, were the necessity of
"dying to live", and inwardness. From within, Jesus taught, come all things that elevate
and that defile a man. And secondly, the name
Modernism has been appropriated by a school
of Catholic thinkers who, with the help of the
pragmatist philosophy, have defended a kind
of Catholicism which has cut itself loose from
the historical facts on which Christian dogma
is based. Truths of faith are said to belong to
a different order from truths of fact, and to be
independent of them. In an age which takes

scientific research seriously, and is not likely
to take it less seriously, I cannot think that
this doctrine of a double truth will make head-
way. It is too obviously the desperate exped-
ient of men who have ceased to be Christians,
but who desire to remain Catholics.

In spite of differences due to temperament
and training, differences which we should wel-
come as signs of independent and vigorous
vitality, the best religious thought of our age
seems to be converging upon Christianity as
the religion of the Spirit. The infallibilities
are gone, the infallible Church as well as the
infallible book. Nor can we trust to the Inner
Light quite as the old Quakers did. They
were in danger of making the Inner Light
itself external, in their anxiety to accept it as
infallible. We do not need these props;
Clement's conception of faith satisfies us. As
for the old proofs from miracle and prophecy,
we now see that, even if the facts could be established, they could not carry the weight
which the old apologetics placed upon them.
A critic of Lord Balfour's *Foundations of Belief* remarked: "It is the peculiarity of theological architecture that the foundations are
ingeniously supported by the superstructure."

We are in fact driven back upon the *Testamonium Spiritus Sancti,* the witness of the spiritual life to itself. And it is enough.

Do I predict that the religion of the Spirit will have a resounding triumph? No, I do not. I can find nothing in the Gospel to justify the notion that the true religion will ever convert the world at large. "When the Son of Man cometh, shall he find faith,—or, the faith,—on the earth?" "If they have called the master of the house Beelzebub, how much more them of his household?" "If they have persecuted me, they will also persecute you; if they have kept my saying, they will keep yours also." "Woe unto you when all men shall speak well of you, for so did their fathers of the false prophets." An uphill fight against heavy odds, or an inward apostasy and unholy alliances,—such is the alternative for the Christian societies, now no less than it was eighteen hundred years ago.

It is, however, possible to predict a rosier political future for Romanism. Mr. Hilaire Belloc, in his history of the French Revolution, argues that the Jacobins made a fatal mistake in antagonizing the Church. The Bolsheviki have done the same, and in twenty years Russia will probably be the most devout, superstitious, and conservative country in Europe. Bolshevism has cut its own throat, and it is probable that the Revolution will before long see the necessity of a *Concordat* with the Black Internationale. That Church can make no terms with communism which is incompatible with family life; but communism is dead anyhow, and there is not much to prevent an alliance between predatory socialism and the Roman Church, based on a common policy of controlling primary education in the interests of their propaganda, of destroying the modern industrial system, and of silencing the voice of science. We must remember that Calvinism, the most robust form of Protestantism, is rather closely allied with business enterprise and material progress. I have shown elsewhere why it is that the modern millionaire, if he is not a child of the Ghetto, is usually a grandchild of John Calvin, Protestantism, therefore, is hated by the Revolution as well as by the Roman Catholic Church, and it is not difficult to argue that Christ would not have approved of modern capitalism.

If this suggestion seems fantastic to optimi*tic Americans, I would ask them not only to read history, which shows that alliances of this kind are highly dangerous, but to study the present conditions in a far more advanced democracy than America,—the Commonwealth of Australia,—and to consider the significance of that sinister figure, Cardinal Mannix.

Nations get the religions that they deserve, and the future of the white races is not secure. But I have not the slightest fear that the light kindled in Galilee will ever be put out. The Spirit of Christ, the same yesterday, to-day, and forever, is "with us all the days, even to the end of the world." Those will follow Him who are not afraid to take up their cross.

CHAPTER I

WHY I AM A CATHOLIC

By

GILBERT KEITH CHESTERTON

THE difficulty of explaining "why I am a Catholic" is that there are ten thousand reasons all amounting to one reason: that Catholicism is true. I could fill all my space with separate sentences each beginning with the words, "It is the only thing that. . ." As, for instance, (1) It is the only thing that really prevents a sin from being a secret. (2) It is the only thing in which the superior cannot be superior; in the sense of supercilious. (3) It is the only thing that frees a man from the degrading slavery of being a child of his age. (4) It is the only thing that talks as if it were the truth; as if it were a real messenger refusing to tamper with a real message. (5) It is the only type of Christianity that really contains every type of man; even the respectable man. (6) It is the only large attempt to change the world from the inside; working through wills and not laws; and so on.

Or I might treat the matter personally and describe my own conversion; but I happen to have a strong feeling that this method makes the business look much smaller than it really is. Numbers of much better men have been sincerely converted to much worse religions. I would much prefer to attempt to say here of the Catholic Church precisely the things that cannot be said even of its very respectable rivals. In short, I would say chiefly of the Catholic Church that it is catholic. I would rather try to suggest that it is not only larger than me, but larger than anything in the world; that it is indeed larger than the world. But since in this short space I can only take a section, I will consider it in its capacity of a guardian of the truth.

The other day a well-known writer, otherwise quite well-informed, said that the Catholic Church is always the enemy of new ideas. It probably did not occur to him that his own remark was not exactly in the nature of a new idea. It is one of the notions that Catholics have to be continually refuting, because it is such a very old idea. Indeed, those who complain that Catholicism cannot say anything new, seldom think it necessary to say anything new about Catholicism. As a matter of fact, a real study of history will show it to be curiously contrary to the fact. In so far as the ideas really are ideas, and in so far as any such ideas can be new, Catholics have continually suffered through supporting them when they were really new; when they were much too new to find any other support. The Catholic was not only first in the field but alone in the field; and there was as yet nobody to understand what he had found there.

Thus, for instance, nearly two hundred years before the Declaration of Independence and the French Revolution, in an age devoted to the pride and praise of princes, Cardinal Bellarmine and Suarez the Spaniard laid down lucidly the whole theory of real democracy. But in that age of Divine Right they only produced the impression of being sophistical and sanguinary Jesuits, creeping about with daggers to effect the murder of kings. So, again, the Casuists of the Catholic schools said all that can really be said for the problem plays and problem novels of our own time, two hundred years before they were written. They said that there really are problems of moral conduct; but they had the misfortune to say it two hundred years too soon. In a time of tub-thumping fanaticism and free and easy vituperation, they merely got themselves called liars and shufflers for being psychologists before psychology was the fashion. It would be easy to give any number of other examples down to the present day, and the case of ideas that are still too new to be understood. There are passages in Pope Leo's *Encyclical on Labor* which are only now beginning to be used as hints for social movements much newer than socialism. And when Mr. Belloc wrote about the Servile State, he advanced an economic theory so original that hardly anybody has yet realized what it is. A few centuries hence, other people will probably repeat it, and repeat it wrong. And then, if Catholics object, their protest will be easily explained by the well-known fact that Catholics never care for new ideas.

Nevertheless, the man who made that remark about Catholics meant something; and it is only fair to him to understand it rather more clearly than he stated it. What he meant was that, in the modern world, the Catholic Church is in fact the enemy of many influential fashions; most of which still claim to be new, though many of them are beginning to be a little stale. In other words, in so far as he meant that the Church often attacks what the world at any given moment supports, he was perfectly right. The Church does often set herself against the fashion of this world that passes away; and she has experience enough to know how very rapidly it does pass away. But to understand exactly what is involved, it is necessary to take a rather larger view and consider the ultimate nature of the ideas in question, to consider, so to speak, the idea of the idea.

Nine out of ten of what we call new ideas are simply old mistakes. The Catholic Church has for one of her chief duties that of preventing people from making those old mistakes; from making them over and over again forever, as people always do if they are left to themselves. The truth about the Catholic attitude towards heresy, or as some would say, towards liberty, can best be expressed perhaps by the metaphor of a map. The Catho-

lic Church carries a sort of map of the mind
which looks like the map of a maze, but which
is in fact a guide to the maze. It has been
compiled from knowledge which, even considered as human knowledge, is quite without
any human parallel. There is no other case
of one continuous intelligent institution that
has been thinking about thinking for two
thousand years. Its experience naturally covers nearly all experiences; and especially
nearly all errors. The result is a map in
which all the blind alleys and bad roads are
clearly marked, all the ways that have been
shown to be worthless by the best of all evidence: the evidence of those who have gone
down them.

On this map of the mind the errors are
marked as exceptions. The greater part of it
consists of playgrounds and happy hunting-
fields, where the mind may have as much liberty as it likes; not to mention any number of
intellectual battle-fields in which the battle is
indefinitely open and undecided. But it does
definitely take the responsibility of marking
certain roads as leading nowhere or leading
to destruction, to a blank wall, or a sheer
precipice. By this means, it does prevent men

from wasting their time or losing their lives upon paths that have been found futile or disastrous again and again in the past, but which might otherwise entrap travelers again and again in the future. The Church does make herself responsible for warning her people against these; and upon these the real issue of the case depends. She does dogmatically defend humanity from its worst foes, those hoary and horrible and devouring monsters of the old mistakes.

Now all these false issues have a way of looking quite fresh, especially to a fresh generation. Their first statement always sounds harmless and plausible. I will give only two examples. It sounds harmless to say, as most modern people have said: "Actions are only wrong if they are bad for society." Follow it out, and sooner or later you will have the inhumanity of a hive or a heathen city, establishing slavery as the cheapest and most certain means of production, torturing the slaves for evidence because the individual is nothing to the State, declaring that an innocent man must die for the people, as did the murderers of Christ. Then, perhaps, you will go back to Catholic definitions, and find that the

Church, while she also says it is our duty to work for society, says other things also which forbid individual injustice. Or again, it sounds quite pious to say, "Our moral conflict should end with a victory of the spiritual over the material." Follow it out, and you may end in the madness of the Manicheans, saying that a suicide is good because it is a sacrifice, that a sexual perversion is good because it produces no life, that the devil made the sun and moon because they are material. Then you may begin to guess why Catholicism insists that there are evil spirits as well as good; and that materials also may be sacred, as in the Incarnation or the Mass, in the sacrament of marriage or the resurrection of the body.

Now there is no other corporate mind in the world that is thus on the watch to prevent minds from going wrong. The policeman comes too late, when he tries to prevent men from going wrong. The doctor comes too late, for he only comes to lock up a madman, not to advise a sane man on how not to go mad. And all other sects and schools are inadequate for the purpose. This is not because each of them may not contain a truth, but precisely because each of them does contain a truth; and is content to contain a truth. None of the others really pretends to contain the truth. None of the others, that is, really pretends to be looking out in all directions at once. The Church is not merely armed against the heresies of the past or even of the present, but equally against those of the future, that may be the exact opposite of those of the present. Catholicism is not ritualism; it may in the future be fighting some sort of superstitious and idolatrous exaggeration of ritual. Catholicism is not asceticism; it has again and again in the past repressed fanatical and cruel exaggerations of asceticism. Catholicism is not mere mysticism; it is even now defending human reason against the mere mysticism of the Pragmatists. Thus, when the world went Puritan in the seventeenth century, the Church was charged with pushing charity to the point of sophistry, with making everything easy with the laxity of the confessional. Now that the world is not going Puritan but Pagan, it is the Church that is everywhere protesting against a Pagan laxity in dress or manners. It is doing what the Puritans wanted done when it is really wanted. In all probability, all that is best in Protestantism will only survive in Catholicism; and in that sense all Catholics will still be Puritans when all Puritans are Pagans.

Thus, for instance, Catholicism, in a sense little understood, stands outside a quarrel like that of Darwinism at Dayton. It stands outside it because it stands all around it, as a house stands all around two incongruous pieces of furniture. It is no sectarian boast to say it is before and after and beyond all these things in all directions. It is impartial in a fight between the Fundamentalist and the theory of the Origin of Species, because it goes back to an origin before that Origin; because it is more fundamental than Fundamentalism. It knows where the Bible came from. It also knows where most of the theories of Evolution go to. It knows there were many other Gospels besides the Four Gospels, and that the others were only eliminated by the authority of the Catholic Church. It knows there are many other evolutionary theories besides the Darwinian theory; and that the latter is quite likely to be eliminated by later science. It does not, in the conventional phrase, accept the conclusions of science, for the simple reason that science has not concluded. To conclude is to shut up; and the man of science is not at all likely to shut up. It does not, in the conventional phrase, believe what the Bible says, for the simple reason that the Bible does not say anything. You cannot put a book in the witness-box and ask it what it really means. The Fundamentalist controversy itself destroys Fundamentalism. The Bible by itself cannot be a basis of agreement when it is a cause of disagreement; it cannot be the common ground of Christians when some take it allegorically and some literally. The Catholic refers it to something that can say something, to the living, consistent, and continuous mind of which I have spoken; the highest mind of man guided by God.

Every moment increases for us the moral necessity for such an immortal mind. We must have something that will hold the four corners of the world still, while we make our social experiments or build our Utopias. For instance, we must have a final agreement, if only on the truism of human brotherhood, that will resist some reaction of human brutality. Nothing is more likely just now than that the corruption of representative government will lead to the rich breaking loose altogether, and trampling on all the traditions of equality with mere pagan pride. We must have the truisms everywhere recognized as true. We must prevent mere reaction and the dreary repetition of the old mistakes. We must make the intellectual world safe for democracy. But in the conditions of modern mental anarchy, neither that nor any other ideal is safe. Just as Protestants appealed from priests to the Bible, and did not realize that the Bible also could be questioned, so republicans appealed from kings to the people, and did not realize that the people also could be defied. There is no end to the dissolution of ideas, the destruction of all tests of truth, that has become possible since men abandoned the attempt to keep a central and civilized Truth, to contain all truths and trace out and refute all errors. Since then, each group has taken one truth at a time and spent the time in turning it into a falsehood. We have had nothing but movements; or in other words, monomanias. But the Church is not a movement but a meeting-place; the trysting-place of all the truths in the world.

THE ROMAN CATHOLIC
HIERARCHY

THE Roman Catholic Church is that branch of the Christian Church which acknowledges the Pope, or Bishop of Rome, as its head. It claims to be the only legitimate inheritance by an unbroken tradition of twenty centuries of the commission and powers conferred by Christ upon the Apostles. It may be divided historically into two periods, the first beginning before the Council of Trent (1541-1563), with an assembly which initiated a fresh attack on the Pope's authority, and extending from about 1431 to 1789; the second reaching from the French Revolution to the present.

After the Reformation in the sixteenth century the Central European nations which had separated themselves from the central unity of the Church prospered materially. The mercantile freedom acquired by Holland, the waning power of Venice and Genoa, the colonial enterprise of Protestant England, the growth of Russia (ultimately involving destruction of the Catholic Kingdom of Poland), the rise of Prussia as a great Protestant State by the side of Catholic Austria,—all these causes tended to restrict the influence of the Roman See.

The seventeenth century saw forces at work within the Church. The number of students in Jesuit colleges alone increased before 1700 to nearly 200,000. The first half of the nineteenth century saw a gradual disappearance of

[31]

bitter prejudice. In England, removal of legal disabilities was the prelude to restoration of the English hierarchy in 1850. In Germany, Catholic revival has been marked. In 1905 the French Government repudiated the Concordat made in 1801 by Pius VII and Napoleon.

At the head of the Roman Catholic Church is the supreme Pontiff Pius XI, Achille Ratti, formerly Archbishop of Milan, elected as successor to Benedict XV and crowned February 12, 1922. The College of Cardinals, made up of seventy members, is the Senate of the Roman Church.

There are at present four American Cardinals: William O'Connell, Archbishop of Boston, Dennis J. Dougherty, Archbishop of Philadelphia, Patrick J. Hayes, Archbishop of New York, George W. Mundelein, Archbishop of Chicago. There are 17 Archbishops in the Roman Catholic Hierarchy of the United States, 98 Catholic Bishops, and 23,159 Priests. Other American Catholic statistics are as follows: churches, 17,146; seminaries, 105; colleges for men, 218; academies for girls, 716; parish schools, 6,388 with 1,988,376 pupils; orphan asylums, 316; homes for the aged, 121. In the World War 814,768 American Catholics were in service, of whom over 16,000 were killed.

The estimated total Catholic population in the United States is 18,559,787. It is of interest to contrast this figure with the totals in other countries as shown in the following table compiled by the Atlas Hierarchicus of Streit in 1913:

WHY I AM A CATHOLIC

Catholic population of	Europe	186,196,342
" " "	America	86,855,097
" " "	Asia and Africa....	13,279,811
" " "	Australia	1,313,610
Total		267,644,860

At present the Catholic population of the world is estimated at 324,328,408.

CHAPTER II

WHY I AM AN EPISCOPALIAN

By

CHARLES LEWIS SLATTERY

Bishop Coadjutor of Massachusetts

IN these days when we often read that earnest men have changed their ecclesiastical allegiance, there is something to be said for any communion when, if a man be born in it, he stay in it to the end. I was born in the Episcopal Church. I have seen attractive gardens on all sides of my enclosure filled with noble people; but I have never had the least inclination to leap any wall or break through any hedge to get out of my own place of privilege and fellowship. I have suspected that if I had been born in some other communion I might have stayed there quite as contented. But I am now thinking only of the fact. I was born in the Episcopal Church and am every day more thankful that all my

[34]

life I have had its nurture. This article is
meant to tell why.

The first quality in the Episcopal Church
which commands my grateful respect is its
sense of proportion. There are a few things
which are held essential both in belief and in
character. Beyond these essentials is a large
liberty. One discovers this sense of proportion by a glance at the Catechism in the Book
of Common Prayer. The Apostles' Creed is
the only statement of faith required of a person to be admitted to the full fellowship of
the Church of Christ. There is not a word
about the way in which the Bible is inspired,
the kind of Ministry which is valid or regular,
the definition of sacraments and other rites,
or the manner of worship,—that is, whether
the clergy shall wear distinctive dress in
church or shall use precomposed forms. All
these are minor matters and are left in a sub-
ordinate place. Even in the creed itself there
is a variety of emphasis; for in the Catechism
the child is asked, after he has said the creed,
"What dost thou chiefly learn in these Articles
of thy Belief?" And we then have the great
answer: "First, I learn to believe in God the
Father, who hath made me, and all the world.

[35]

Secondly, in God the Son, who hath redeemed me, and all mankind. Thirdly, in God the Holy Ghost, who sanctifieth me, and all the people of God."

So in character, the Church depends on the duty towards God and the duty towards one's neighbor as the summary of the ancient law approved by Christ himself. The child says the commandments; but their real meaning for him is in Christ's summary. He must so live that he will show his love to God and his love to his neighbor. There will be excellent men all about the Episcopalian, even some within his own Church, telling him that, if he were as strict as they are, he would observe the rule never to dance, or never to play cards, or never to eat meat on Fridays. If the Episcopalian has any Christian manners at all he will not discount the value of such rules for those who are helped by them, but he will say that he has a harder responsibility. He has certain great principles, and with the help of these he must decide what is right for him, what will make him truly love and serve God, what will make him a true and loving servant to man. If dancing or card-playing dulls his spirit, makes him worldly, selfish, bad, he will have nothing to do with them. If they are innocent diversion and help towards the freedom of the serious moments, when they come with their strain, then he may, just so far and no farther, use them. He has to decide. If fasting on Fridays makes him kinder, more sympathetic, firmer in self-discipline, he would wisely use it. If it is a mere form, making him Pharisaical, unpleasant, snappish, he had better eat more meat on Fridays than any other day in the week. The petty rule may help or hinder. He has a greater responsibility.

This sense of proportion is so bound up with the genius of the Episcopal Church, that it is the subject of taunt as well as of praise. Emerson mockingly said of us, "By good taste are ye saved." I suspect that he knew that there was some truth in his jest. Balance, discrimination, wise choices are fundamental in fine character. On the other hand, one remembers George Tyrrell's advice to a member of the Church of England who contemplated going over into the Roman communion: "No," he said; "don't come; you would not be happy. The Church of Rome tells you what you must do at every turn. The Eng-

lish Church makes you decide for yourself.
Having had that freedom, you could not endure the constraint which would be put upon
you." Though Tyrrell had chosen the Church
with rules, he saw the high advantage of
freedom and poise, determined by the full responsibility of the individual.

Another quality in the Episcopal Church
which commands my gratitude is its sense of
continuity. It feels its organic relation to
the distant past. It speaks reverently of the
doctrines of the Apostles which have been
cherished through all the Christian centuries;
it commands its clergy not to teach anything,
as necessary to salvation, but that which they
shall be persuaded may be concluded and
proved by the Scriptures; it steadfastly believes that the ministers of the Church have
not only the direct call of the Holy Spirit,
and so are immediately appointed, but that
they are also commissioned by those who were
themselves commissioned; these in their turn
being regularly ordained by those formerly
accredited; and so on back to the days of the
Apostles. There is no word of exclusion here,
no attempt to judge others; but there is profound satisfaction in the remembrance that

the Episcopal Church is conscious of a continuous history reaching through the ages to those who saw the Lord Christ face to face.

We sometimes hear people say that the Episcopal Church began in the days of Henry the Eighth. If that be true, then the Church of Rome began about twenty years later at the Council of Trent. Both the Church of Rome and the Church of England dwell on a continuous past. At the time of the Protestant Reformation there was a Counter Reformation. It is absurd to say that one part of Christendom remained fixed and the rest was reformed. There was, by common necessity, a reformation all along the line. Luther, Calvin, and John Knox as well as Cranmer and Ignatius Loyola felt the roots of their faith and practise deep in the soil of the past. Each was striving to regain the primitive purity and glory of the Church as Christ had inspired it and would then inspire it. Each was trying to get away from the moral corruption, the disfigurement, and the superstition. Some of the reformers were breaking away from this part of the immediate inheritance, others from other parts, but all were, consciously or uncon-

[39]

sciously, trying to retain and secure the best of all that had been since the day of Christ.

It is specious to say that only those parts of Christendom which maintain that they have a connection with the earlier Church do have it; for others are by their life and their faith evidently the fruit of that earlier Church. But it is an honorable trait in a Christian communion that it should be aware of its history, and value it. We Episcopalians are glad that our ministry has a continuous history; we are glad to think that Anselm and Francis of Assisi and Boniface and Augustine of Hippo and Athanasius and Clement of Alexandria are our direct spiritual ancestors. There have been reformations again and again in the two thousand years; other reformations will necescarily come if the Church maintains vigorous life. True reformations do not break continuity, they restore continuity. As Churchmen have often pointed out, the old stone tower at Newport did not cease to be when the vines were taken away from its stones. It had a different aspect, but it was more itself than ever, because men saw at length its reality. So the Church was not a new Church at the Reformation, but a Church restored by the removal of recent growths which had concealed its true and continuous life.

A third quality in the Episcopal Church for which I am grateful is the Book of Common Prayer. Like all great possessions the Prayer Book is easily abused. Its wealth of devotion may be employed carelessly and mechanically. Its prayers may be gabbled or rattled through with gross, though unintentional, irreverence; and no advantage may be taken of the large freedom which the Church intends its officers to use, especially by the present well-considered revision. By such stupid carelessness the Prayer Book becomes a burden and a grief: the most halting or the most diffuse extempore worship is better. (And at all times the merits of extempore prayer must never be forgotten.) But when a reverent and intelligent minister, by diligent preparation, has determined just what the arrangement of the service shall be, and then leads a congregation in the worship of God by means of the Book of Common Prayer, I know that the beauty, dignity, and simplicity so touch the heart that true worship is induced, and the whole life of a congregation is given to God. The familiarity of the words, when they are freighted with association, when they are direct and appealing, is itself a help, provided the human voice, really praying, puts into them the life of to-day. Like the greatest music, the ancient prayers awake one's deepest emotions, just because they are well known; one waits for the phrases and the petitions as one waits for the remembered harmonies in music, and the spirit uses them as wings to mount into the heavenly spaces.

Once more, I value the Episcopal Church because its government in this country is thoroughly democratic, almost exactly parallel with the provisions of our political constitution. This is quite natural because, when the Nation became independent of England, the Church became independent also. And, very largely, the same men who framed the constitution of the Nation framed the constitution of the Church. Thus as we have in Congress, the Senate and the House of Representatives, so we have in the General Convention, the House of Bishops and the House of Deputies. As a Governor and a Legislature govern a State, so a Bishop and a Diocesan Convention govern a Diocese. A Diocese has a certain amount of self-direction, but it is

also directed by the General Convention.
Corresponding with the local township is the
Parish governed by a Rector and a Vestry,
who are elected in turn by the people of the
parish. These same parishioners in parish
meeting elect (or delegate their Vestry to elect
for them) representatives to the Diocesan
Convention. The Diocesan Convention,—
made up of the Bishop, all the clergy of the
Diocese, and the laymen thus elected from the
parishes,—elects four clergymen and four laymen to represent the Diocese in the General
Convention. Further, on all important matters the clergy and the laity vote separately.
Nothing may be done from which a majority
of the lay delegates in either Diocesan or General Convention dissent. The bishops and
clerical deputies in General Convention might
vote unanimously for a certain change in the
Constitution or in the Prayer Book, but unless
a majority of the laymen voted for it there
would be no change. The bishops, moreover,
are constitutional rulers. Their rights and
their duties are rigidly defined. They are
servants of the people, and rule by influence
and love rather than by any mechanical power
vested in them. No bishop for example may

be out of his diocese for more than three months at a time without the formal consent of the Standing Committee of the Diocese.

These are dreary details, but to repeat them seems the only way to make clear what a fundamentally democratic institution the Episcopal Church is. The layman is forced to take responsibility, and his ample rights are clearly designated. Many are the times that the laity have saved the Church from hasty and unwise action. And, again and again, laymen have been developed, through this responsibility, to become leaders in the thought and advancing life of the Church.

Men sometimes say that this democracy of the Church is fictitious, because they know a diocese where the bishop is an autocrat and allows in his diocese no convictions or usage other than his own, or because they know a parish where a rector insists on his own type of service, and drives the sturdiest parishioners out of his church. Thus, to such critics the Episcopal Church is made to seem narrow, unsympathetic, hard. I am sorry for this. Often such leaders have not long been in our communion or in our country, and so do not understand the genius of the Episcopal

Church in America. There is a loving-kindness and breadth in the tradition and life of the Church which distinguishes its permanent character; and no unfortunate expositions, here or there, can destroy it.

Christ said, "By their fruits ye shall know them." The genuine test of the value of any group of Christ's followers is, "What have they done? What are their fruits?" Of any Christian Church, when we frankly face the judgment of Christ, there is only one fruit which, we recognize, can satisfy Him. This is not a mighty organization able to control millions; it is not imposing buildings rising on every country hilltop, and on the chief square of every city; it is not wide and convincing scholarship and an array of unquestioned credentials. These all have their place; but the Lord of the Church, as we read His life in Palestine, evidently cared little for them. The test of any community, confessing Him, is Christlike character. If it cannot show power to create that, all the trappings and all the historical accuracy and assurance of the universe cannot make it a true Church.

I believe in the truth of my communion because, through my lifetime, I have seen it to be the means by which Christ has created character like His own. I have seen haughty and impatient people become tender and thoughtful of the feelings and needs of all about them; I have seen selfish and bitter people turned into happy, self-forgetting servants of their kind; I have seen dishonorable people, stained with grievous fault, made into saints; I have seen people, mocked by failure and pain and bereavement, rise from their trouble to be leaders of joy and peace. And I know that the love and worship and personal ministry of the Church have, through God's mercy, been the medium of this transformation.

Not for one moment am I fool enough to think that the Episcopal Church has any monopoly in this supreme achievement in life. I exult in the saints of other communions whom I have known; they are examples which prove the source of their strength. It may be that some communions of the Church create more saints. All I need to know, so far as my direct allegiance is concerned, is that I am absolutely sure that the Episcopal Church does bear that sort of fruit.

One sometimes hears that the Episcopal

Church is the Church of the rich, and that although Episcopalians do much to help the poor they do it in the spirit of condescension. The great middle, working class has, it is said, little place in it. Now it chances that I have served parishes in different parts of the nation, and to-day I am serving all the parishes in one diocese. I think I may speak from direct knowledge. The Episcopal Church is serving all kinds of people, and the parishes I see and know are loving brotherhoods in which rich and poor, and all the grades between, are as one family. I once served one of the most prosperous parishes in America. I suppose an outsider thought it only for the exclusive and the rich. Everyone looked well-to-do. But I, who put the bread of the Holy Communion into the outstretched palms, saw many and many a hand hard with manual toil or stained with the humble tasks of the home. Christ, through the Church, had given all these people a light and a beauty in their faces which made one forget the accidents of the ways they earned their living. The very order of the worship made people careful to come to church in suitable dress: those who had "king's clothing" came in simple garb, those who had little came in their best. It is a law of good taste. There are vulgar, pretentious, patronizing people everywhere; so there will be Episcopalians foolish enough to be pleased that their Church is called the Church of the rich. They are feeding their pride on a lie. It is, if anything, to-day the poor man's Church; but the poverty which Christ commended is not worn to be seen of men.

There is only one other quality of the Episcopal Church which I shall mention. I believe that, if it honestly will live up to its vision, it has important contributions to make to the ultimate unity of the Church. From time to time, members of the Church fret over its name. It is confessedly a very awkward name,—"The Protestant Episcopal Church in the United States of America." Men ask, Why don't you call yourselves the name you use in the Creed, "The Holy Catholic Church"? The simple answer is that we are not the Holy Catholic Church. We hope and pray that we are part of it, but only all Christian people, baptized in the Name of the Father and of the Son and of the Holy Ghost, are the Holy Catholic Church. Definitions of limits will vary, but we stand close to the Christ whom men saw in Galilee, if we make the limits inclusive rather than exclusive. Our name is not beautiful, but I trust we shall keep it till, with other Christians uniting into one great whole, we, with them, shall deserve the complete name.

No other community of Christians includes so many temperaments and tastes bound into the loyalty of its life as the Episcopal Church. We have the extremes of ornate ceremonial and of chaste simplicity; of literal interpretation and of very free interpretation; the Quaker and the Roman Catholic seem to meet in the same pew. Conviction rubs against conviction; preference against preference; form against form. But there is unity of spirit; and with it, a common desire to remain in one enclosure. We then say, if we can do it, all can do it; let us find the essentials which are the life of all loyal Christian men and women, and then let the freedom of Christ breathe into us charity, whereby we may dwell together in one organic body, for the good of men, for the glory of God.

I could never say in any creed, I believe in the Episcopal Church. I believe always in the Holy Catholic Church, whose members are now scattered abroad under different names; and I pray that my branch of that whole, by its character and its love towards all men, will do its full share in bringing everyone who calls Jesus Lord and Saviour into the single fellowship of the one Church of the Living God.

THE PROTESTANT EPISCOPAL CHURCH

THE Episcopal Church is the body legally known as the Protestant Episcopal Church in the United States of America. In the words of Bishop Slattery, "it is the daughter of the Church of England, which traces its history back to the early missionaries who came long before the days of Augustine of Canterbury. It did not start new in the sixteenth century, but freed itself then from foreign control." Thus the Episcopal Church claims unbroken continuity with the earliest Christianity.

In America, as the Church of England, it was established in Virginia in 1607. As a separate ecclesiastical body in the United States, it dates from 1789, when it adopted its constitution, in the same hall which had witnessed the framing of the Constitution of the United States of America two years before.

WHY I AM AN EPISCOPALIAN

The movement to constitute one Episcopal Church for the whole United States began in 1784. The "General Ecclesiastical Constitution of the Protestant Episcopal Church in America" was ratified in 1789. It contained provisions for the clerical and lay representation from the church in each State, and it embodied the doctrine and adopted the liturgy of the English Church so far as consistent with the changed political condition.

For twenty years its energy seemed to have been exhausted by its organization. It suffered the unpopularity of identification with the English Church. But after the Convention in 1811 the Church took a vigorous start whose impulse has been felt ever since. It was due chiefly to three men,—Bishops Hobart of New York, Griswold of New England, and Channing Moore of Virginia. In 1817 some Western States were organized into dioceses, and in 1820 the Church was organized in all the original States. A distinctive feature of the middle nineteenth century was the expansion of the Church, which by 1869 was coextensive with the boundaries of the United States. In 1872 there was a separation of a few churches from the main body, which later became the Reformed Episcopal Church. This is less ritualistic in its ceremonies.

The constitution of the Episcopal Church is in many particulars analogous to that of the nation. In legislative matters, the General Convention is supreme. It meets triennially and is composed of the House of Bishops and the House of Clerical and Lay Deputies. On the first of this year the offices of Presiding Bishop and President of the Council were merged under the former title. The present incumbent is the Most Reverend John Gardner Murray, D.D., Bishop of Maryland.

In 1923, missionaries in the domestic field numbered 607 men, 119 women, and a native staff, including Indians and Negroes, of 91. Foreign fields included Latin America, Liberia, and the Orient. There were 408 American missionaries of whom 220 were women, and a native staff of 1880. Expenditures of the Department of Missions in 1923 amounted to $2,682,891, of which $1,- 059,430 was devoted to foreign work. In 1924 there were 8403 churches, 6150 ministers, and a church membership of 1,142,532; 6000 Sunday schools with a membership of 492,436; and $36,935,658 was raised for church purposes. The department of religious education of the Church sponsors a number of educational institutions including two schools of arts and sciences, two nonsectarian colleges, and fourteen theological seminaries.

CHAPTER III

WHY I AM A PRESBYTERIAN

By

HENRY SLOANE COFFIN

Pastor of the Madison Avenue Church

I AM a Presbyterian by inheritance. My forebears, on both my father's and mother's side of the family, belonged in this part of the Church of Christ, and I was thus "fore-ordained". My training in home and church was along Presbyterian lines. I was given a thorough education in the contents of the Bible, committing many chapters and verses to memory, and I grew up with a genuine relish for the things associated with religion. I early learned by heart the Shorter Catechism of the Westminster Divines, which is an excellent mental discipline in its logical reasoning and rhythmical English. Many of its formulations are obsolete, and I am not passing it on to another generation, but its purpose, to supply Christians with definite convictions and to make them think for themselves, is part of the inheritance worth striving to maintain.

When I came to prepare for the ministry, the Church in this country had been troubled by a heresy trial in which the less educated and more intolerant elements had attacked and driven out Professor Briggs. Partly from the Scottish traditions of my family, I began my preparation in Edinburgh, where Scotch Presbyterianism was then, as it still is, much more open-minded and modern than most of the theology taught in this country. The findings of science both in evolution and in historical criticism were taken for granted. The views of the Bible, now labeled "fundamentalist", were not held thirty years ago by any accredited leaders in the Scottish Kirk. It was assumed that, while religious experience was a continuous factor in human life, and generation after generation men repeated their fathers' discoveries of God, their interpretations of them varied with changing views of the universe. The Westminster Confession of Faith, which is a standard of the Churches of Scotland, as well as of the Presbyterian Church of this country, was viewed as an historic expression of the beliefs of Christians in the Seventeenth Century, which modern ministers were expected to subscribe only in the sense that they accorded with its main convictions and stood in the same devout succession.

I completed my course in Union Theological Seminary, which I found certainly not one whit less orthodox than the Scottish halls of divinity, and where a similar view of the Church and her creeds was inculcated. I presented myself for licensure in the Presbytery of New York, where the large majority impressed me as an open-minded and open-hearted company of Christian leaders, apparently sympathizing with the outlook on truth and life in which I had been trained.

I remain a Presbyterian, not because I believe that the Presbyterian Church is better than any other, but because I owe to it whatever religious inspiration I possess, and because I believe that in it for the present I, with my ancestry, training, and temperament, can most usefully serve the Kingdom of God.

And the Presbyterian Church has certain advantages as an instrument for furthering the cause of Christ in our land:

One is its historic constituency. Presbyterianism is the form which the Church at the Reformation assumed in France, Switzerland, The Netherlands, Scotland, Hungary, Bohemia, in large parts of Germany, and among the majority of Puritans in England and Wales. The elements in our population from these stocks form the large mass of the membership of the Presbyterian Church, and they are a sturdy, thoughtful, conscientious, and devout fellowship, who make strong churches and push the missionary enterprise vigorously at home and abroad. Few churches expect and receive more from their people.

A second is its breadth. Those who framed its constitution were not thinking of setting up a sect, but of providing an organization for the entire body of Christians, the Holy Catholic Church of Christ, within a given nation, and in fellowship with the Church throughout the world. Doubtless their performance came short of their avowed intention, but their aim is beyond question. No creedal tests are exacted of its communicants, and it welcomes to its membership everyone who is trying to live as a follower of Christ. Congregations who desire it employ the Apostles' Creed in public worship; but its acceptance is not required for Church membership. Indeed in most congregations the invitation to the Lord's Table is given to all who love Jesus Christ and are seeking to follow Him. Ministers and other office-bearers are required to accept the Scriptures as the supreme standard of faith and life and the Westminster Confession "as containing the system of doctrine set forth in the Holy Scriptures." Such subscription was not originally intended by the Westminster divines, and I hope to see the day when it will no longer be required.

A third is its adaptability. Each congregation is free to arrange its own form of worship and methods of work. Some Presbyterian churches are fairly ritualistic, others extremely informal; some have elaborate music, others sing Gospel hymns. The tradition in worship is one of simplicity, but there is nothing to prevent a congregation employing a liturgy or using symbolic forms, where such are found helpful. In many congregations historic prayers are in use as well as the prayers which the officiating minister offers in his own phrases. A church in a cosmopolitan centre, seeking to meet the needs of various types of people, must present the community with several differing kinds of worship, and this a Presbyterian church is at liberty to do. Nor is there any prescribed uniformity in method of work. In the city of New York, no communion offers greater contrasts in its activities than does ours in two such churches as the Labor Temple and the Fifth Avenue Church. Both are Presbyterian.

A fourth is the combination of local freedom with a unifying organization, placing behind every congregation the guidance and backing of the whole communion. Presbyterianism, as is well known, played no small part in the shaping of our national Constitution, and in the Church it provides for home rule and centralized leadership. In the Church, as in the nation, this is effected by adjustments and compromises which seem at times unsatisfactory to some of those interested, but the result is a large measure of liberty for each congregation and for each presbytery, with a strengthening sense of the fellowship and oversight of the whole Church. Each minister is ordained by a presbytery, and the ministerial succession goes back in a continuous line through the ages to the apostles. But it is not this succession through the laying on of hands which is stressed, but the continuity of the Church of to-day with the Church of New Testament times by the possession of the apostolic Spirit of faith and hope and love. Presbyterianism has organized itself nationally, like other Churches which reshaped their constitutions at the Reformation, but it relates these national churches to one another in the Alliance of Reformed Churches, which represents some forty-eight million adherents throughout the world.

A fifth is its intellectual tradition of religion as an experience not merely to be felt, but also to be interpreted. It has always stressed a thorough Biblical education for its members, and takes pains to train younger and older people in its Sunday Schools and Bible classes. Not every Presbyterian is "mighty in the Scriptures"; but if he is not, he is aware that he does not come up to the standard of his Church. Its ideal of a sermon is one which both instructs and edifies. Presbyterians, when they go to church, wish to learn something and to come away with a clearer under-

standing of God's will for them. It is not by
accident that the Presbyterian Church, perhaps more than any other, has come into public notice by its doctrinal discussions. It is the
genius of our communion to attempt to explain its faith. This involves forming definite
opinions, and men with opinions inevitably
differ. So long as these doctrinal discussions
are not carried into Church courts, with the
attempt to oust those whose views are not
shared by the majority, they are praiseworthy
efforts to ascertain truth, and they enlighten
the Church. When they turn into heresy
trials, they cease to have any value as means
of discovering truth, and become painful exhi-
bitions of bigotry. Most heresy trials are
hideous blunders.

A sixth is its practical contribution towards
Church unity. Presbyterians do not talk so
much about Church unity as do the members
of some communions, but one rarely finds a
movement where various churches are com-
bining for evangelism or on the mission field,
or in building up an interdenominational institution like the Y. M. C. A. or the Y. W.
C. A., where Presbyterians are not whole-
heartedly coöperating, and often leading.

An element of ecclesiastical weakness is the amount its members give to causes outside its immediate work,—a weakness often deplored by those entrusted with the raising of the income of our various missionary and benevolent boards, who claim that our people are afraid to give to anything labeled Presbyterian lest they seem sectarian in their interest. But it is surely a laudable frailty on our part. We always cordially invite to the Lord's Table members of other churches, and we recognize the ordination and ministerial standing of the clergy of all evangelical churches. They are welcomed to preach in our pulpits, to share in the administration of the sacraments, and, if called and admitted to serve as pastors in our congregations, they are never re-ordained.

Presbyterians have much to be proud of in the work of their Church in our own country and in many lands. Those who have been reared under its teaching, even when they cease to be actively connected with its fellowship, speak of their "Presbyterian consciences", and the Presbyterian conscience is a robust and sensitive ethical monitor. Communities under Presbyterian influence are

[61]

God-fearing, law-abiding, intelligent, and independent. Indeed if I am ever disgusted with the narrowness or the crass stupidity of some ecclesiastical assembly,—and we have our full quota of retrograde leaders,—I think of the goodly company of pastors and missionaries and Sunday School teachers, and Church workers of many types, and tell myself that they are the real Church, and not the official utterances of some reactionary Assembly or the doings of some ecclesiastical politician.

But it is only fair to say that I am a Presbyterian in spite of certain tendencies which crop out in our Church from time to time. One is the notion that the Presbyterian Church is a denomination, and not an attempt to embody the Catholic Church of Christ, and a denomination which is held together by agreement in theological opinions. Historically we in this country derive our constitution from Commonwealth Britain and from Scotland where a national Church was contemplated, embracing in its membership every sincere Christian and admitting to its ministry every man deemed fit to be a clergyman in any Christian Church. But one hears a certain type of

Presbyterian saying: "I consider so and so a useful minister of the Gospel, but I don't think he belongs in the Presbyterian Church." Such folk conceive of our communion as a sect within the Church, and not as an attempt to provide a fellowship for the whole Body of Christ. I take issue with that position both on historical grounds and as a matter of Christian principle. I have no interest in sectarianism; or rather I have no interest in it save to fight it to the death as opposed to the mind of Christ and to the Church of the New Testament. I believe that it is our duty to enlarge the scope of our services and work so that we render our communion homelike to every follower of Jesus, and to remove every restriction which impedes any minister of Christ from exercising his God-given calling within our Churches. To acknowledge that a man possesses the Spirit of God and is equipped to serve the Kingdom, but to hold him unfit to minister in our select theological club because he does not wholly share the views of the majority, seems to me perilously like blasphemy against the Holy Ghost. I am a Presbyterian in the historic sense of that word,—one who believes in a Presbyterian polity inclusive enough to comprehend all followers and ministers of Christ, who are willing to work and worship in its fellowship.

A second is the strict interpretation of the vow required of ministers and other office-bearers, in which they accept the Bible as "the Word of God, the only infallible rule of faith and practise," and receive the West-minster Confession of Faith "as containing the system of doctrine taught in the Holy Script-ures." Those who are familiar with our his-tory and know the various interpretations which have been given to this vow, can take it sincerely and yet be modernly minded Christ-ians; but the language is archaic, is not under-stood by the public, and acts as a barrier to many who would be valuable ministers and leaders in the Church. At the present mo-ment a so-called "fundamentalist" group has been trying to place a literalist construction upon this vow, and to insist that any state-ment to be found both in the Scriptures and in the Confession of Faith may be made obligatory by action of the General Assembly upon candidates for the ministry. Should this thoroughly unprotestant view prevail, the Church will inevitably be broken into two sections, as it has unhappily been several times in the past, and few men of university education will be found entering the ministry of the reactionary section. While this controversy has been going on in our theologically uncultured land, Scotland has taken an advance step, and its United Free Church has so modified the formula of subscription as to render it acceptable to most evangelical Christians. I find myself a Scotch Presbyterian *con amore*, and I cannot help wishing that our American Church may not long remain less progressive than the Scottish Kirk.

So I may say finally that I am a Presbyterian only temporarily. The name carries many hallowed memories and associations, but it seems to me to belong to the past rather than to the present. It connotes primarily a particular mode of Church government. Time was when it was thought that one might discover in the New Testament the creed, the polity, and the worship of the Church divinely prescribed for all ages. We now know that this is not the case. The New Testament contains various doctrinal interpretations of the faith,—half a dozen views of the atonement and several explanations of the origin of the

Person of Christ. It contains various types of Church organization, which sprang up in accordance with the usage in different localities. There is no indication that Christ ever gave His Church either a creed or a constitution, and no hint that the forms of government adopted by groups of Christians in the first century were meant to continue indefinitely. All that Christ was interested in giving his followers was His Spirit. The Spirit would guide them into truth, and would lead them in organizing to fulfil their task. St. Paul thought of the Church not as following the precedents of an accepted constitution, but as equipped and directed by the present Holy Spirit. Episcopacy, Congregationalism, Presbyterianism are names derived from modes of Church government. Each has its strengths and weaknesses, and each points back to germinal beginnings in the Church of the New Testament; but none is more apostolic or more of divine institution than the others. The Church of to-day and to-morrow may well try to combine the proved good points of all three in her organization.

As a matter of fact it is not easy to discover the distinctive characteristics of our existing

Protestant communions. The advantages
which I have ascribed to the Presbyterian
Church will all doubtless be claimed by others
for their own churches. For nearly twenty-
two years, on the faculty of an inter-denomi-
national theological seminary, I have tried to
teach future ministers of all leading communions, — Baptist, Congregationalist, Disciples, Episcopalian, Lutheran, Methodist, as
well as Presbyterian,—and I know that the
work for which these men were preparing
themselves is the same. Our denominational
divisions do not stand to-day for differences
in teaching or in the type of Christian life produced. There may be differences in emphasis,
but these are trifling. There are radicals and
reactionaries, high, low, and broad churchmen, in all communions, and the denominational lines are not real frontiers. Ministers
have more in common with the clergy of other
churches who have had an education similar
to their own than with fellow-ministers of
their own church with a different training.
Our people pass readily from a church of one
communion to that of another. There are
genuine differences,—the difference between
the infallibilist type who believe in an iner-

rant book or an unerring pope, and the experiential type who believe in the progressive leadership of the Spirit within. But these types are found side by side in every Protestant communion and to some extent even in Roman Catholicism.

In attempting to meet the religious needs of our time it is quite impossible to think in denominational terms. A rural community cannot have an adequate school of religious education where its children are divided among several small churches. There is no distinctively Episcopal interpretation of the Gospel for international relations and no peculiarly Methodist message of the application of Christian principles to industry. The missionary problem, both in this country and throughout the world, cannot be satisfactorily answered save by the combination of all our Christian forces. The perpetuation of our meaningless divisions means inefficiency, waste, and the continued impoverishment of Christians by their separation from their rightful comrades in thought and worship and labor. Once granted that no existing church is specially gifted with true doctrine or correct orders or the only valid mode of administering some sacrament, and that all have valuable historical heritages and large present contributions to make to the united Church of Christ, it ought not to be impossible to arrive at some form of organization which would combine liberty and unity, conserving the values in our differences and making possible the gains of united life and service.

Already just across our northern border, Methodists, Congregationalists, and Presbyterians are consolidated in the United Church of Canada. The time is ripe for a similar and even more inclusive organic union among the churches of the United States. I hope to live to see it, and I am ready to do my utmost for its accomplishment. Meanwhile I remain a Presbyterian, resolved to seek to end any barriers in our communion which render it less comprehensive than the United Church of Christ should be.

THE PRESBYTERIAN CHURCH

PRESBYTERIANISM was not an attempt to organize a new church, but to reform the Catholic Church of Christ along New Testament lines. Its chief

[69]

leaders were John Calvin in Geneva, and John Knox in Scotland, and the movement led by Calvin linked itself with the earlier attempts at reform by John Huss in Bohemia and Peter Waldo in Italy. The Confession of Faith and Form of Government in use throughout the English-speaking churches were framed by the Assembly of Divines which met at Westminster in 1643.

Presbyterianism reached this country through colonists from Puritan Britain, who organized a church as early as 1640 at Southhampton, Long Island. Later it was augmented by colonists from Scotland, North Ireland, The Netherlands, Huguenot France, and parts of Germany; more recently by those from Hungary and Czecho-Slovakia. The first Synod was formed in 1729, and the first General Assembly in 1789.

There are many branches of the Presbyterian Church in the United States. Among the largest are The Presbyterian Church in the U. S. A., The Presbyterian Church in the U. S. (so-called Southern Presbyterian), The United Presbyterian Church, The Reformed Church in the U. S. (formerly known as Dutch Reformed), The Reformed Church in America (formerly known as German Reformed).

As one of the three principal systems of ecclesiastical polity known to the Christian Church, Presbyterianism occupies an intermediate position between Episcopacy and Congregationalism. In Episcopacy the supreme authority is a diocesan bishop; in Congregationalism it is the members of the congregation assembled in church meeting; in Presbyterianism it is a Presbytery or council composed of ministers and elders representing all the churches within a specified district. The Presbytery chooses its Moderator each year from among its ministerial members. His duty is to see that business is transacted according to Presbyterian principle and procedure. The Moderator has no special power or supremacy over his brethren, but is honored and obeyed as primus inter pares.

Appeals and complaints may be taken from the Presbytery to the Synod, which is a provincial council consisting of ministers and representative elders from all the congregations within a specified number of Presbyteries. In case settlement here is not final, further appeal is had to the General Assembly, representing the whole church.

Presbyteries vary in size and extent. A city Presbytery like New York covers only Manhattan and Staten Islands. The sparsely settled State of Nevada is a single Presbytery. The average Presbytery covers eight or ten counties and has thirty or forty churches and 6000 communicant members. The Synod corresponds roughly in area to a State, and contains a minimum of three Presbyteries. The General Assembly, called at least once a year, is the national body. At present there are in this country 299 Presbyteries, 46 Synods, 10,017 ordained ministers, 47,986 elders, 9649 churches, 3,181,801 communicants, and approximately 6,000,000 adherents. Throughout the world there are approximately 60,000,-000 communicants and adherents.

The Present Moderator of the General Assembly for the United States is the Reverend Charles R. Erdman of Princeton Theological Seminary.

CHAPTER IV

WHY I AM A LUTHERAN

By

NATHAN SÖDERBLOM

Archbishop of Upsala

AM I a Lutheran? Certainly I am a
member of the One Holy, Catholic, and
Apostolic church. That Church of God is
found in most countries, even in Sweden, yea,
it forms the very soul of our nation, according to the words of Gustavus Adolphus anent
"the majesty of the Realm of Sweden and
God's Church that dwelleth therein."

I, myself, and my fellow-believers fully
accept St. Paul's spiritual and universal faith,
—but we do not call ourselves Paulinians.
We fully accept the divine authority of
Christ, proclaimed sixteen hundred years ago
by Athanasius at Nicea,—but we do not call
ourselves Athanasians. We fully accept St.
Augustine's personal experience of God's

supreme sovereignty and human impotence in salvation,—but we do not call ourselves Augustinians. We fully accept the wave of love which reached even our distant country in the Franciscan revival of the thirteenth century, —but we do not call ourselves Franciscans.

We fully accept the message of Evangelic trust and freedom entrusted by God to his prophet Martin Luther, the mightiest genius of religion after St. Paul. But Martin Luther vehemently forbade his friends to call themselves after him, whose body would soon become a sack of worms. They should call themselves simply Christians and by all means not after his mortal name.

In the second generation of the Reformation in Sweden, under a young king who had through his mother become a Roman Catholic, and under the regency of his uncle, a sympathizer with the mitigated Heidelberg faith, the free Council of Upsala of 1593 endorsed the Evangelic Lutheran creed in all its most authentic and explicit form. But no official document in our Church calls us or our Communion, Lutheran. We call ourselves simply the Church in Sweden. But the use of the name of Martin Luther for our section of the

Church has become a custom and an historic necessity.

Why am I a whole-hearted member of that section of the Church of God?

First of all, I was baptized as a child in the Christian Communion. No human understanding can distinguish the moment when the work of the Spirit begins in the soul of the child. Therefore the Church carries the baby to Christ, beginning its initiation into the mysteries of God's revelation and the Christian life.

Just as every one of us enjoys the accumulated treasures of civilization in a special country and is and becomes a member of humanity through an enlightened patriotism, so also the Christian is introduced into the spiritual world and the communion of Saints, that is, into the realm of Reality and Truth, in being, first unconsciously, then little by little consciously, introduced into the genuine tradition and spiritual deposit of his own section of that Universal Church, and he is appurtenant to the Universal Church in proportion as he is a loyal citizen in his own religious fatherland.

Baptism implies a pledge: "baptizing them

and teaching them to observe all things whatsoever I command you." "I realized only
later in life that the pledge is not equally understood and fulfilled by every section of the
Church of God. I had always taken it for
granted that every child in our Western civilization learned to read and write and know
other useful things as I myself and all Swedish children did. And it puzzled me to hear
later that this was not at all the case. Whence
the difference? Seeking the answer, I found:
Martin Luther and Reformation.

Nothing impressed my childish mind more
in Church and in home than the singing of the
hymns, which gave wings to imagination and
devotion. Asking why such worship, which
enveloped and elevated even the mind of a
child, is not found everywhere, the answer was
the same: Martin Luther and Reformation.

I was seized by the grandeur of the Bible,
read in Home and School and Church in our
own Swedish tongue and penetrating our
literature. Whence that knowledge of the
Bible? Answer: Martin Luther and his
disciples in Reformation.

Sitting at the great Christmas high mass,
awe-struck in the twelfth century Parish

Church with its mediaeval paintings, sculptures, monuments, while the priest, who was my father, worshiped in alb and chasuble before the altar and in his high tenor intoned in the pulpit: *War kristtrogen fröjde sig,* I had no idea that Evangelic Christendom did not accept such venerable and beautiful forms of worship everywhere. Why that reverence? Answer: Martin Luther.

My mother was my first teacher and the best one I ever had. Parts of Martin Luther's Small Catechism were rather hard to learn by heart. But earlier than my memory goes, I have always felt a thrill in my soul when repeating or hearing Martin Luther's confession of his faith in Jesus Christ. I knew later that that piece of literature has been called the most perfect sentence in the German tongue. It runs: "Jesus is My Lord, Who has redeemed me, a lost and condemned creature, secured and delivered me from all sins, from death, and from the power of the devil, not with silver and gold, but with his holy and precious blood, and with His innocent sufferings and death; in order that I might be His, live under Him in His kingdom, and serve Him in everlasting righteous-

ness, innocence, and blessedness: even as He
is risen from the dead, and lives and reigns to
all eternity."

After studies in philosophy and philology
at the University of Upsala, where every matter studied threatened to take my entire mind
and life, I went over to the study of theology.
Hebrew and Greek are compulsory, because
servants of the Church must be able to go
to the sources and make a literary research
according to the revolutionary rule of humanism, applied to the Bible with more consist-
ency by Lutheran than by Erasmus. The
study of Religion is put into the full daylight
of research and scholarship in that seeking
for truth in all domains of existence that char-
acterizes a free University. Such is the
principle, even if shortcomings hide it. Understanding later on that such a rule for training the Ministry is not applied everywhere, I
asked why I was brought to it, and the answer
came again: Martin Luther and Reformation.

Analogous experiences are familiar to
everyone. If they imply depreciation of other
forms of faith and worship and Church organization, they are unworthy of the Christian

name. The divine and eternal truth cannot
be grasped in its entire fulness by the human
mind. The Apostle writes: "I know in
part." If any section of the Church claims to
know perfectly, it repudiates the testimony of
the Apostle. White light is broken into many
colors. In the same way the different sections
and directions in the Church of God ought
not to boast nor to despise each other, but to
contribute with their own purified gifts to
the whole of Christianity.

Every one is dependent on the spiritual soil
from which he emerges. Only the superficial
mind, which never penetrates into the depths
of human life, is more or less independent of
its own origins. If some one underrates his
own spiritual fatherland, if he does not try
to see and appreciate what he owes to his education and surroundings, he sins in lack of
gratitude to his Creator.

If I try to sum up a definite answer to your
question, I might say in the first place that I
owe to my section of the Church an over-
whelming sense of the greatness of God's free
grace as granting forgiveness and peace to the
troubled human heart and saving men from
perdition, not through their own perishable

endeavors and observances and works, but through faith in Jesus Christ.

From this three seeming antinomies are derived:

I—In our Faith freedom and service are closely united. The thesis of Luther in his "Treaty on Christian liberty" runs: " A Christian is the freest Lord of all things, subject to no one." That he is through trust in God. His confidence, his faith frees him from fear. He fears nothing and nobody except the One Fearful who is God. Trust delivers him from submission to the world, to evil, and to other men. "The one who has a gracious God, should he not break through mountains of copper no longer mortal, but living already here the eternal life?" Thus trust in God creates the superman.

But at the same time the Christian is defined by Luther as "the readiest servant submitted to all." That he is through love. Because he can love God only in his fellowmen. Love becomes the passion of his life and makes him eager and thankful to serve with all the spiritual and material means that God has trusted to him.

Such service is not indiscriminate and ar-

bitrary, but each Christian must serve in his
own vocation, he must build up all his human
relationships, his civic activities and the work
of his soul and body unto the living and
organic Unity that is his calling. Faithfulness in that calling makes life and work
sacred. The entire human existence thus becomes a service, a worship in the house of
God.

II—I have mentioned the high appreciation, some say the overvaluation of knowledge
and studies, in authentic Lutheranism and
Calvinism. We believe in serious research,
in profound thought and clear-cut doctrine.
And the personal message has an important
place in our worship.

But beside the pulpit which unites us with
our brethren in Evangelic Christendom, we
have in our sancturaries an altar, which unites
us *mutatis mutandis* with our brethren in
Orthodox and Roman Christendom. (Both
pulpit and altar are found also in Anglican-
ism.) The altar means adoration and mystery. The altar and the sacrament of the altar
means that human understanding is unable to
grasp the mystery of salvation. There is a
place in our common worship as well as in

theology, where the reason recognizes its inability and falls down in adoration. No sect in Western Christendom outside the Church of Rome has accentuated in its doctrine the Real Presence and the mysterious communion of the Sacrament as has our Evangelic Lutheran sect, although our faith repudiates any quasi-rational magical explanation of the virtue of the Sacrament.

III—The third seeming antinomy unites tradition and freedom. If we have kept time-honored usages and forms in worship, Church ornaments, and organization, that does not mean any allegiance to nomistic or legalistic religion; on the contrary, it is due to a consistent application of Christian freedom. For freedom does not always mean opposition. It is not often realized that the so-called Lutheran faith has no more genuine characteristic than a perhaps sometimes mistaken but sincere and consistent repudiation, in the name of Evangelic faith and freedom, of any form more brutal or more refined of the religion of law. Not even forms and customs described in the New Testament are considered by our Communion as rules for the future. No law can instil life. The principle of faith and love has to be applied under the guidance of God freely to all human conditions, and to all domains of religion and life.

That chief doctrine was ever and ever again preached by our evangelist Olaus Petri, an indefatigable herald of the grace of God through Christ, and at the same time a humanist. His younger brother, Laurentius Petri, was during more than forty years Archbishop of Upsala, the first of my predecessors after the reformation. Consecrated by Bishops who were themselves consecrated by a Bishop duly consecrated in Rome, he held "apostolic succession" in the common sense of that word, the true meaning of which has been once and forever explained by Dr. Arthur Headlam, now Bishop of Gloucester. But his genuine apostolic succession is proved more intimately by the following rule in his Church Ordinance of 1571, which belongs to the symbols or confessions of the Church in Sweden. He says that the enemy pretended earlier that ceremonies and vestments and customs were necessary for salvation, although they were indifferent and sometimes contrary to the pure Evangel. Now, he adds, the same enemy attacks us from the other side, telling us that we must for the sake of salvation abolish venerable customs and destroy church ornaments and vestments and customs. Although many of them are adiaphorous or irrelevant to the Faith, some are dear to the Christian people. No statement can prove more clearly the idea of Christian freedom than this characteristic reverence for things that have become dear to our forebears and that are not contrary to the Evangel.

To be named after Martin Luther is contrary to the prophet, who in the sixteenth century restored and fulfilled the golden line of Evangelic faith and mystical communion with God in St. Paul and St. Augustine and others. But when a section of the Church must have a name of its own, if we cannot keep to the admonition of the Apostle in the third chapter of the First Corinthians to name ourselves only after Christ, I should myself prefer the method criticized in the same chapter. In Corinth they named themselves after St. Paul or after Apollos or after Cefas. Some sections of the Church of Christ are named according to their forms of organization,— Papal, Episcopal, Presbyterian, Congregationalist; others are named in accordance with their special forms of piety,—Baptists, Methodists; some are named after a place or a country, such as Roman, Greek, Anglican. If a special sect-name is necessary, it might be taken from one of the great servants of God and Christ, since the unspeakable richness and mystery of religion is more easily apprehended in a human life than in any formula or doctrine. Thus Augustinian, Benedictine, Franciscan, Calvinist, Wesleyan are to me, I dare say, expressive names so far. Shall I repeat that, as far as I can see, the history of religion has no genius after St. Paul equal to that of Martin Luther?

Perhaps such a custom of using the names of heroes and saints for subdivisions of the Church can bring into it a more correct idea of Christian perfection. Perfection and holiness are too often regarded in a negative sense as lack of faults and sins, instead of in a positive sense. When in consecrating saints, Rome attributes an essential and perhaps the most essential importance to miracles operated by the candidate, that means a primitive conception of religion, which seems to me incompatible with Christianity. But it is at the same time a very strong and wholesome correction

[84]

of the current Evangelic opinion, because it means that sanctity and perfection are regarded as the outcome and testimony of divine power, not as the absence of more or less conspicuous human imperfections. Faults are obvious in Martin Luther. He often repudiated any attempt to make him a saint. But to come to his writings from those of the great experts of mystical exercises is, as a brilliant devotee of mystical religion wrote to me, when to his astonishment he discovered Martin Luther, like coming from the air of a hot-house to a well of fresh water. Luther was devoured by a passion for peace of soul and divine truth.

If we call ourselves or are called by others by the name of one of those heroes of Christian faith and communion, they all with one voice ask with the Baptist to look not at themselves nor at ourselves, but at Christ, and they invite us with St. Philip to come and see Jesus of Nazareth. Thus overcoming the sectarianism and the too human boundaries of our traditions and conceptions, they oblige us to feel united around the Cross, the supreme symbol of divine grace and human faithfulness.

THE EVANGELICAL LUTHERAN CHURCH

THE Evangelical Lutheran Church had its origin in the Reformation under the leadership of Martin Luther, who believed that he was restoring the stream of New Testament Christianity. Expelled from the Roman Hierarchy by the Anathema of the Pope in 1521, Luther disclaimed the Pope's authority to separate him from the Church of Christ and began his mission as a reformer in the spirit of St. Augustine, St. Francis, Wycliffe, and many others. Since his day the faith which bears his name has spread to the ends of the earth, and falls into three main groups,—(1) Evangelical Germany with her neighbors, Poland, Russia, Lithuania, Czecho-Slovakia, Austria, Hungary, Roumania, Jugo-Slavia, France, Holland; (2) a group of northern nations which have established the Lutheran Church as the State Church: Denmark, Iceland, Norway, Sweden, Finland, Esthonia, and Latvia; (3) the United States of America, which counts twelve million adherents. In other parts of the world Evangelical Lutheran groups are also found, and the total (between eighty and a hundred million, with about seventy thousand congregations and forty-nine thousand pastors) comprises the largest confessional body in non-Roman Evangelical Christendom.

The Lutheran Church emphasizes Christian education. Its central fundamental doctrine is justification by faith alone in Jesus Christ. Its confessional position is indi-

cated in a statement drawn up at the Convention of Lutherans from twenty-two nations held at Eisenach two years ago: "The Lutheran World Convention acknowledges the Holy Scriptures of the Old and New Testament as the only source and the infallible norm of all church teaching and practise; and sees in the Lutheran Confessions, especially the Unaltered Augsburg Confession and Luther's Small Catechism, a pure exposition of the Word of God."

Lutherans were present in the earliest American colonies. A Lutheran Christmas service was held on Hudson Bay, 1619, and a Lutheran congregation was formed on Manhattan Island in 1648. Early Swedish and German immigrants planted churches in Pennsylvania, Delaware, Virginia, the Carolinas, and Georgia, and Luther's Catechism was translated into the languages of the Virginia Indians in 1646. The first Synod was organized in Pennsylvania in 1748, and a General Synod was organized in 1820. To-day there are seven general Lutheran Church bodies in the United States and Canada with a communicant membership of 2,457,017 and thirteen smaller general Lutheran bodies, using predominantly the English language in services, although the Gospel message is brought to the people in sixteen different languages.

The Lutherans of the United States and Canada have 16,406 churches; 10,799 ministers; 2,622,554 communicants,—and constitute the third largest Protestant Church in this country. There are more than 60,000,000 enrolled Lutherans in Europe; 5,000,000 in North America; 500,000 in Asia; 400,000 in Africa; 300,000 in South

TWELVE MODERN APOSTLES

America, 350,000 in Oceanica. In other words, Lutheranism represents about 47 per cent of Protestantism, 14 per cent of Christendom, and five per cent of the world population.

CHAPTER V

WHY I AM A BAPTIST

By

 EDGAR YOUNG MULLINS

President of the Baptist World Alliance

I CAN group the reasons why I am a Baptist under two general heads. The first is heredity and the second is a reasoned conclusion.

My father was a Baptist minister, and his father was also a Baptist minister. The families on the sides of both my father and mother have been Baptists through several generations. It was, of course, not likely that I would escape being a Baptist if I became anything religiously. At the same time, however, it is pertinent for me to say that I did not become a Christian until I was in my twenty-first year and, according to the Baptist way, up to that time had no connection as a member of any church. I was taught in the principles

[89]

of right living by my parents. They sought to win me to the Christian life. But there was not the slightest effort on their part to coerce my action or to influence me to a premature decision. In fact there was one period during and following my college career when I became skeptical on several points of Christian teaching. All along, however, there was a conflict between my intellectual questionings and my religious yearnings. My conscience was keenly alive and the fundamental need and demand for religion was always present. Strange as it may seem, it was in the period of intellectual doubt that I was converted. I use the old-fashioned word because it best describes my experience. The preacher,— the late Major W. E. Penn, a layman in fact and lawyer-evangelist,—preached the Gospel in a meeting in the First Baptist Church of Dallas, Texas, in a way which made a powerful appeal to the religious side of my nature. Without any emotional cataclysm of any kind I yielded my will to Christ. The moral and spiritual reënforcement which followed this act completely transformed my purposes and plans.

There was no effort on the part of the

preacher to meet my intellectual difficulties in a formal way. These were for the time being in abeyance. My awakening was spiritual and religious. But my act of surrender to the will of Christ produced a new attitude toward my intellectual problems and difficulties. These were simply transcended by the new spiritual experience. The problems on the intellectual side seemed to be far less important than they had been. They were afterwards considered, of course, but I saw them in the context of my new spiritual life and had comparatively little trouble with them. I was profoundly impressed with the fundamental truth that on their intellectual side the problems of religion are insoluble apart from a genuine religious interest. There is no conflict with reason in a man's religious experience. But the experience introduces new facts and data with which reason works. One discovers that in the effort to intellectualize religion without religious experience or interest the major premise is lacking.

It was after my conversion that I began to consider the reasons for being a Baptist. My father had taught me years before that it was of the essence of becoming a Baptist that one

should know why. He said that to accept
what Baptists taught merely in imitation of
others, even of one's own parents, was not in
keeping with the spirit of the Baptist faith.
One became a Baptist, he insisted, as a result
of one's own personal and free choice, based
upon an intelligent consideration of the reasons behind the act. And this brings me to
the reasoned conclusions to which I referred
at the beginning of this article. In outlining
them I shall necessarily have to draw some
comparisons unfavorable to other forms of
Christian life and belief. But this implies no
bad spirit on my part and no desire to claim
a monopoly of excellence in my own particular beliefs. What I say is rather a testimony
to my own inner life and mental processes
which best meet the requirements of religion
as I know it.

First of all, I am a Baptist because, as I see
it, the Baptist interpretation of Christianity
best conserves the freedom of faith. Baptists
relate the individual to Christ in a free and
spiritual way. The teaching concerning
Christ is not a dogma imposed by authority.
It is not subscription to a creed. We accept
the deity of Christ along with His humanity,

not by authority, but by discovery. We find Him as Saviour from sin and freely exalt Him as Lord of our lives. His lordship is a great formative principle in all our thinking. But it is a lordship which has come to us by way of experience of His Grace working in us.

In applying for membership in a Baptist church faith in Christ and acceptance of His lordship is the prime condition. Subscription to an elaborate creed is not required. The desire to know the will of Christ and willingness to obey it is the cardinal qualification. This implies a change of heart, commonly called the new birth. A new disposition has been imparted by the Holy Spirit as the penitent surrenders to Christ in an act of faith.

Baptists accept the authority of the Scriptures in the same free way. By the testimony of the Scriptures themselves and by the response of their own spiritual life they find that the Scriptures are the word of God. But there is not and has never been any authoritative declaration or formula promulgated by Baptists as to the inspiration and authority of the Scriptures. They accept these not because early church councils decreed them, or a papal declaration established them, or because the Reformation movement was based upon the authority of the Bible as against the authority of the papacy. Many modernists try to get rid of the authority of the Bible by stigmatizing belief in it as bibliolatry. The term "bibliolatry" may be applicable to some mechanical theories of inspiration by which men attempt to define that authority in such a way as to make of the Bible a sort of fetish. But Baptists do not arrive at their view of the authority of the Scriptures in any such way. The Bible, for them, is a spiritual authority. It becomes such an authority by a spiritual process in which the whole religious nature of man is active, and in which the self-authenticating power of the Bible is felt. It is also a free intellectual process in which reason is illumined by faith.

A similar explanation applies to the way of Baptists in the matter of creeds and confessions of faith. No central authority speaks for Baptists. Their churches and district associations usually announce certain cardinal truths of Christianity in order to define themselves. But these are never imposed on others. They are merely testimonies to the way in

which the Bible is understood and interpreted. They are not identical in meaning,
although there has been remarkable unity
among Baptists until comparatively recently.

From the preceding it seems to me quite
evident that the Baptist attitude to truth is
the scientific as well as the Christian attitude.
This is not the attitude of negation or destruction. It is rather the attitude of openness of
mind and heart to spiritual truth. Spiritual
reality can only be known by those who are
open to it. If Newton had prejudged the
power of gravitation he would have failed in
his effort to formulate its law. Men who prejudge Christ will never discover him as Saviour and Lord. Men who prejudge the Bible
by preconceived critical theories or philoso-
phies will never be able to appreciate and
value it. Some of the most perfect specimens
of logic to be found in current theological literature are the books which approach the discussion of the Bible with such theories and
preconceptions. They make so slight an impression on the public mind because men unconsciously realize that the fundamental attitude is wrong. A false major premise vitiates
all the reasoning. The perfect logic rises

from a false foundation. The average man, or in the hackneyed phrase "the man on the street" knows that logic of this kind is special pleading. He recognizes and feels and knows that the Scriptures are not the sort of literature which is alleged.

The true Baptist asks for no artificial props for faith. He knows that Christianity is rooted in history. And he insists on the historical element. But he asks for no artificial bolstering up of the historical records. What he stands against is a narrow scholarship which prejudges the records, and a narrow type of religious experience which leaves out the deeper elements in man's nature. In the New Testament Christ was preached as risen Saviour and Lord. This preaching created a new spiritual world and the literature known as the New Testament. This process can be reproduced, indeed is being reproduced, in its essential features to-day on a grand scale. But it is not a repeatable process unless the spiritual forces are allowed fair play. Men sometimes say that nothing should be held as historically necessary in religion except those things which are repeatable to-day. This is the result of confused thinking. There is no way to repeat the resurrection of Christ from the dead; and yet it was the foundation of early Christianity and is historically provable. The preaching of a crucified, atoning, and risen Christ saves men from the power of sin and transforms them morally and spiritually, individually and socially. There are thousands of demonstrations of this in our country every Sunday, and in fact every week day in the year.

I am a Baptist because Baptists insist strongly upon the rights of the individual. Personal choice is the basis of discipleship with them. We regard the practise of infant baptism, for example, as inconsistent with the freedom of the individual. We think it right to train the growing child until he can choose for himself. Proxy faith and personal faith are contradictory ideas.

"But," some one may ask, "is not this individualism a dangerous principle? Where will you draw the line?" The reply is that in one sense there is no line to be drawn anywhere because Baptists believe in absolute religious liberty for all men everywhere as will appear later. Among themselves, however, the corrective principle is the lordship of

Christ. It is this lordship which unites Baptists in a coherent body. Along with it is loyalty to the New Testament, because in it Christ appears in the record of His historical manifestation.

The value of the principle of individualism is self-evident when we look at history. For centuries the individual was repressed. He was smothered in the corporate life, ecclesiastical or political. Huss, Savonarola, Luther, Galileo, William Carey, Roger Williams, and many others are instances. If God speaks directly to men, then men should be permitted to declare God's message.

Again the objector says: "How will you curb the license of one group and the fanaticism of another group? Both imagine or claim that they are speaking for God. Does not your principle convert the Baptist denomination into a free-lance club?" Here again the answer is not far to seek. Loyalty to Christ and the Scriptures is the corrective. There would be no room for a Nietzsche among Baptists because he declared that Christ's teachings are the morality of slaves and that Jesus was a curse to mankind. Nor could Baptists well receive the philosopher who said recently that the world has outgrown Christ, since Christ offered Himself as a spiritual authority to men. His view was that all authority is outgrown or transcended. Baptists stand or fall on the authority of Christ as the revelation of God.

The principle of individualism leads to democracy in church polity. The direct relation of the soul to God imposes responsibilities and confers rights upon all believers. Churches should, therefore, be self-governing bodies.

Baptists also insist upon a regenerate church membership. Self-government in polity requires intelligence and character. This is one reason why Baptists so insist upon individual and personal choice, and the direct relation of the soul to God. These are the guaranty of spiritual life. And spiritual life must precede wise judgment in spiritual matters. Democracy in church government and a regenerate church membership, therefore, are indissolubly bound together.

Two points are worthy of emphasis here, points on which Baptists are often misunderstood by others. One is that Baptists are chiefly concerned to maintain the outward forms of Christianity, baptism and the Lord's supper. The other is that Baptists ascribe a saving power to baptism. Both these impressions are entirely wrong. Baptists have always stressed the fact that baptism is a symbol, not a sacrament, as is also the Lord's supper. Neither has any saving power. Salvation is a spiritual fact, not a sacramental process. A man is saved by faith in Christ alone. With us one joins the church and is baptized because he has already been saved and not in order to be saved. Baptism is an outward dramatic representation of a preceding spiritual change. Water is a symbol of cleansing or regeneration. Submersion is a symbol of spiritual death and burial. Emergence from the water is a symbol of resurrection from the dead. Thus the form of the ordinance, immersion, is necessary to express the spiritual meaning. To destroy the form is to destroy the meaning. But the form is absolutely without saving power. Christ commands the form. It is useful as a portrayal in vivid outward fashion of great spiritual truths. Baptists observe the form as an act of obedience to Christ's command, and not in order to be regenerated or saved. Baptists attach less importance to the ordinances than any Christian denomination except the Quakers. They do maintain immersion as the Scriptural form of this ordinance. The scholarship of the world is practically a unit as to this as the original mode of baptism. But we value it for its symbolism, not for any saving power residing in it. The late Robert J. Burdett explained why he was a Baptist as follows:

I love the beautiful symbolism of the ordinances of our baptist church; I love a baptism that does not have to be argued, defended, or explained but is in itself such a living picture of burial and resurrection that even the blind eye must close itself if it would not see. And I love the creed that is written nowhere save in the New Testament, which allows growth and the changes which must come with increase of light and stature without periodical revision. If there wasn't a Baptist church in the world there would nevertheless be millions of Baptists in every generation. I love the democratic churches. I even resent the innovation of "advisory boards" in the Baptist churches. And I love the Baptist recognition of the right of "private judgment," the liberty of personal opinion. I love the free responsibility of the human soul, standing on a level platform face to face with God, with no shadow of pope, or bishop, or priest, or man-made creed falling between himself and his Master. That's why I am a Baptist.

I am a Baptist because Baptists are and
have ever been strong advocates of religious
liberty. All Americans now accept this doctrine theoretically. Baptists in Virginia and
Rhode Island fought for it when State
churches were the vogue. Their's is the anti-
thesis to the Roman Catholic system at most
points and yet Baptists stand for the rights of
Roman Catholics in their religious life. They
stand even for the rights of atheists to their
beliefs about religion, although, of course, regarding them as radically wrong in those beliefs. No human power, political or ecclesiastical, has any authority over the individual
conscience. Religion is a matter between God
and man. The State has no authority in the
religious sphere. Equal freedom for all religious beliefs and equal protection to all is
the Baptist ideal. Legislation favoring one
denomination or one religion more than
others is foreign to the Baptist conception.

Out of this religious right grows all other
human rights,—intellectual, economic, civic,
and social. It is the direct relation of man to
God which is the basis of them all. The free
human personality can find itself, realize
itself, come to its own in all spheres under the

operation of this principle. Thus it inevitably becomes a social principle of the most fruitful kind. Human duties accompany human rights. And it is in a society where men recognize both duties and rights that the Kingdom of God comes.

Democracy in the church, which is simply an extension of the principle of individual rights, is the primary social expression of it. It is astonishing how local self-government in the churches lends itself to the expression of Christianity as a spiritual religion. Baptists have no ecclesiastical courts to try heretics. Hence they have rarely been divided into warring groups over heresy trials.

Democracy in church government fits well into any just form of political government. This statement is well illustrated in recent Baptist growth in Russia. In 1914, Baptists in Russia numbered about one hundred thousand. To-day they are variously estimated from two to five millions. A competent observer has said that this growth in Russia is "the most remarkable spiritual phenomenon in modern times." Even under Soviet rule they have increased almost beyond belief. One of the chief causes of the growth has been the spirituality and democracy of the Baptist interpretation of Christianity. They hold that the Church has no political function. Hence the State does not fear them. The freedom and independence of the congregations make it impossible to mobilize them for political action. If they had a human authority over them, they might be used for wrong ends and the State would justly fear them. History teaches the sad lesson that centralized ecclesiastical systems may be perverted to political uses and ends. Baptists seek to avoid this abuse.

Baptists believe that there are great basic principles underlying New Testament Christianity. They are universal and self-evident truths. Some years ago I stated these truths in the form of axioms as follows:

First, the theological axiom: The holy and loving God has a right to be sovereign.

Second, the religious axiom: All souls are equally entitled to direct access to God.

Third, the ecclesiastical axiom: All believers are entitled to equal privileges in the church.

Fourth, the moral axiom: To be responsible the soul must be free.

Fifth, the religio-civic axiom: A free Church in a free State.

Sixth, the social axiom: Love your neighbor as your-self.

To the above I would now add,

Seventh, the civic axiom: The sovereignty of the State resides in the citizen.

These axioms may be reduced to one great universal principle which expresses the historical attitude of Baptists: the competency of the soul in religion under God. Baptists oppose all systems which concentrate responsibility in the hands of any class or group, whether they be priests, bishops, or other ecclesiastical officials.

These principles are at the foundation of the whole Baptist conception of Christianity. We believe they are universal and comprehensive enough to stand permanently as the expression of the fundamental meaning of religion. They are in the highest degree in harmony with the scientific spirit and with all the great ideals of civilization and principles of human progress.

Baptists are a great spiritual democracy possessing both the excellencies and the faults of such a body. An article by a writer in an iconoclastic American magazine recently painted the Baptists in lurid colors. Occasionally the writer does give a fact, but most of the article is reeking with animosity and and abounds in false statements. He was not looking for the truth about the Baptists. He went to the Baptist garbage barrel and selected specimens to his taste and spread them on the pages of the magazine. If he had entered the front door and observed the Baptist household he would have painted a different picture. He would have found many of the wealthiest and most cultured along with many that are poor. He would have found a people strong in the city as well as the country. He would have found first class as well as second and third class schools. He would have found broadminded men of vision as well as reactionaries. He would have found remarkable unity as well as diversity. He would have found genuine tolerance as well as the narrow intolerance he so much emphasizes. In short this writer, if he had eyes to see, would have found a great spiritual democracy, full of virility and high purpose, inspired by a common vision of righteousness, debating and discussing and sometimes wrangling over points of difference, struggling with poverty and abounding in wealth, advocating some foolish things but in the main committed to great constructive ideas,—in a word, he would have found a people full of life and health in spite of many faults, and inspired by high ideals and a common purpose to serve God and humanity.

THE BAPTIST DENOMINATION

*B*APTISTS *began with the churches of the New Testament. They are not Protestants. They flourished down to the uniting of Church and State by the Emperor Constantine and continued through the Middle Ages in secluded parts of Europe. They existed under various names, always, however, maintaining certain Baptist characteristics.*

Baptists appeared in the United States under the leadership of Roger Williams. Williams, banished in 1635 from Massachusetts for his Baptist views, settled at Providence, R. I., where the first Baptist church in this country was established. It was through him that the charter was secured establishing Rhode Island as the first State guaranteeing religious freedom to all people. Separation of Church and State has been one of the outstanding contributions Baptists have made to our American civilization. Historians have attributed many of Thomas Jefferson's governmental conceptions to the fact that he frequented assemblies in a small Baptist meeting-house near his home in Virginia. Baptists in Virginia presented the petition to President George Washington that resulted in the first amendment to the Constitution of the United States.

William Carey, an English Baptist, founded modern missions in 1792; Adoniram Judson, an American Baptist, inaugurated the missionary movement in America in 1812; other eminent Baptists are listed as follows: John Milton, author of Paradise Lost; Daniel Defoe, author of Robinson Crusoe; John Bunyan, author of Pilgrim's Progress; Charles H. Spurgeon, most popular preacher of modern times; Alexander Maclaren, prince of expositors; Henry Dunster, first President of Harvard, the oldest American university; Warren G. Harding, late President of the United States; Charles Evans Hughes, former Secretary of State; Dwight Filley Davis, present Secretary of War; David Lloyd George, former British Premier; John D. Rockefeller, Sr. and Jr., and many others.

Baptists have no hierarchy, no creed. Grouped together in a given community for New Testament purposes they form a church. These churches unite within small geographical boundaries in district associations; in States as State Associations; in the South as the Southern Baptist Convention; in the North as the Northern Baptist Convention; in Canada as the Canadian Baptist Convention; in England as the British Baptist Union. Baptists of the world have the Baptist World Alliance with Dr. Edgar Young Mullins as President.

WHY I AM A BAPTIST

The following chart gives some recent statistics:

United States	Churches	Members	Sunday School Pupils	Ministers
Northern Baptist Conv.	8,519	1,368,967	1,098,873	8,315
Southern Baptist Conv.	27,919	3,574,531	2,219,975	16,790
Others, incl. Negroes....	21,473	3,802,072	1,086,020	19,499
Other Countries..............	9,768	2,647,540	1,023,009	15,133
Grand Totals..........	67,679	11,393,110	5,428,277	59,737

CHAPTER VI

WHY I AM A QUAKER

By

RUFUS MATTHEW JONES

Professor at Haverford College

THERE must be two stages in this story. The first will deal with the past tense, and the second with the present tense. In the first brief section I shall tell why I *was* a Quaker, and in the second, I shall explain why I *am* one, for "am" does not necessarily follow "was."

It seems to me that there is no mystery quite so deep as the mystery of birth. How we begin, why we begin, gets no answer from anybody. But, once more, why we emerge just precisely *when* we do emerge and why we come into the peculiar environment and locality which becomes our habitat,—of all that there is plumb ignorance. I might have "come" any time within an odd million of years and I might have "parked" anywhere from Kamchatka to Tierra del Fuego, but I arrived in the second half of the nineteenth century and I came to life in a little hamlet in Kennebec County, Maine.

Plato used to thank the gods for having made him human instead of a brute, a man instead of a woman, a Greek instead of a barbarian, but most of all for permitting him to be born in the time of Socrates. I feel a similar thanksgiving that I was born in that particular spot, at the moment when the little group of Quakers who lived there were at their highest point of moral and spiritual life. Next to heredity, if it be not in fact equal to it in importance, is the formative influence of the social group upon the individual life. It is as important, as indispensable, as the air one breathes. My uncle was, just at the time when I was growing up, one of the foremost Quaker preachers in America, and two of my aunts were among the "prophets" or "prophetesses" of our faith. My mother was a living transmitter of grace and truth. It was, too, the period of itinerant Quaker ministry and so the most gifted Quaker preachers both in England and America came one after another to our community, usually to our home. Through them and through the great messages of my uncle, I drew upon the best spiritual vintage which the Quakers had to offer.

The home is always the supreme nursery of religion. It not only furnishes ideas for the growing boy, but, what is vastly more important, it forms his subconscious life, the subsoil of all his thinking and of all his sentiments. Here in this country home with its stream of Quaker guests and with its own heavenly atmosphere I was *bred* a Quaker. This faith became as much a part of me as my own bone and muscle were.

Then when the time was ripe for it, I went to a great Quaker School. Like my own local community, this school happened just then to be at its very best from the point of view of Quaker influence. It gave me both mental culture and spiritual outlook. From its noble idealism I went on to three years of life in a Quaker College. Here at Haverford I had as my most important teacher, a scholar and a saint, Pliny Earl Chase. He taught me philosophy and ethics, but his personal friendship, his interest in my future, and his intimate intercourse with me far outweighed any-

thing he taught me, and from the first he stood
forth as my ideal of a Quaker. It was at his
suggestion and under his influence that I first
began to study the great mystics and wrote
my graduating thesis on Mysticism. Through
these college years, I was meeting the finest
living specimens of the Quaker faith and I
was discovering its best and purest aspects.

A year abroad, with open sesame introduc-
tions, brought me into contact with many of
the significant Quaker leaders in England, including John Bright, and I came back to teach
for six years in the two Quaker schools of
New England. During this period I became
personally acquainted with the Quaker poet
Whittier, and his religious teaching became
thereafter a major influence with me. With
this preparation I became editor of a Quaker
weekly periodical and at the same time an instructor at Haverford College. Every step
of my earthly life had woven tighter the spiritual web in which I was swaddled as a baby.
I could have shed my skin more easily than
I could have sloughed off my ancestral faith.
And yet I would drop it this minute if it did
not fit and tally with my whole intellectual
outlook and if it did not ring true with all

which, with mind and spirit, I hold as truth. Before giving my own confession of faith I want to say emphatically that I hate sectarianism in all its forms and that in writing this article I have no desire to glorify the small religious body to which I belong. I am interested mainly in a life and spirit which ought to become universal and which can flourish not only in the Society of Friends but also in every other denomination and communion of the far-flung Christian family.

I am ready now to tell why I *am* a Friend, a Quaker, to use the old name of reproach. I feel happy and congenial as a member among Friends because they, more than most Christians, I think, lay the main stress upon the cultivation of the inner life. They have endeavored to reduce religion to its essential traits, to an uttermost simplicity. They believe supremely in the nearness of God to the human soul, in direct intercourse and immediate communion, in mystical experience, in a first-hand discovery of God. Their worship is arranged to further as much as possible this immensely important business. They encourage in every way possible individual responsibility in all that concerns and pertains to the religious life. They feel that religion is as much an affair of a man's own personal life as his digestion is. They insist that each person ought to be captain of his own soul and to do his own worshiping for himself, that everyone ought to feel the joy, surprise, and wonder that come when the soul discovers the meaning of fellowship with a Great Companion. What they call "the priesthood of all believers" is the theory that every Christian ought to find his way into a holy of holies and ought to come back with a sense of dedication to reveal and interpret Christ to men. There are a multitude of ways of carrying on this ministry, and any way is a good way which makes God seem more real and which tends to produce in any one a clearer vision of what true life and spiritual service mean. The more natural, that is to say vital, it is made, and the more simple it is, the better and more effective it will be. The Quaker way of silence and the freedom for everyone to share his experience or his personal need help very much to cultivate this simple, natural religious life and tend to deepen the interior life of the individual. There are many other aspects of worship and public service, no doubt, which are important and desirable aspects and which Friends perhaps too much neglect, but this central aspect is, I feel sure, worth all its costs of personal effort and devotion.

To think of religion as a normal function of life, like the beating of the heart or like healthy breathing is, I am convinced, the right attitude, and it is an attitude which forms a pure and wholesome atmosphere for little children to grow up in. If we expect to produce and nurture strong, four-square lives, persons of straight-forward purpose, breadth of human sympathy, depth of character, and upward reach of living experience, we must encourage quiet communion, personal fellowship with God, and a fitting sense of individual responsibility for the soul's highest welfare. Pure, simple, undefiled religion is an immense factor in the highest culture. It refines the life and spirit, it adds grace and beauty to the character, and it makes joy, radiance, and service spontaneous and natural.

Then, again, I like the Quaker way of life. It emphasizes sincerity in word and deed. It calls for a transparency of life that lets every spectator see your motive and purpose and read your heart as though it were an open book. It cares intensely for simplicity,— simplicity in dress, in speech, in manners, in eating and drinking, in recreation, in fact, in all human relationships, especially in that highest relationship of the soul with God. But the most important feature of the Quaker way to life is the settled intention to prac- tise love. There have been endless debates about the moral value of compulsion and about the efficacy of non-resistance, but while the debates run on, the Quaker quietly goes forth on his venturous way of making a posi- tive experiment of that supreme force in the universe, the force of a loving, understanding, coöperating spirit. He believes in justice and he is eager to widen the area of justice among men, but he feels convinced that there is a practical working method far superior to jus- tice, the method of entering into mutual rela- tions of understanding one another, of suffer- ing together, of giving and sharing, of chang- ing the whole level of an issue by bringing grace and love into operation. It is in very truth a holy experiment, and it works on hu- man souls as the sun of the vernal equinox works on the ice of rivers and on the frozen clods where vital seeds lie buried.

This way of life is made more effective through certain deep convictions which most Friends take very seriously indeed. It is, first, a great Quaker conviction that there is something divine in man,—a seed of divine life planted in his soul. This conviction gives rise to another, that it is worth while to do humanitarian work even at great cost and effort, because men are dowered with immense spiritual possibilities and they have something within themselves which answers back responsively to trust and love and confidence. The Quakers act, again, on the central conviction that conscience in man's soul is unspeakably august and authoritative. It seems to them like a compass needle for discovering the right direction in the most transcendent matters of life as well as on occasions that are common and trivial. These convictions tend to bring forth still another conviction closely related, that when once a truth or duty becomes clear and plain, it must be followed and obeyed undeviatingly and without compromise. The insistence on the straight path, the refusal to wind or wabble in affairs of truth and righteousness, have been noteworthy traits in Quaker history and biography.

Another thing I like about Quakers is their practical principle that religion is something to be *done*, not a pious theory, or a creed in a book, or a set of notions to preach about. When a revelation breaks in on their lives or a truth of divine import dawns upon them, they take it for granted at once that somehow life must square up to that truth. It must march on its feet and go into vital circulation. It must take on flesh and blood and work as a living force in a man's life. They do not care much for the spectator-theory of truth,—that it is something to be observed and rapturously viewed as an object. Nor do they approve the feeling-theory, that truth is something which produces emotional thrills. Truth is not really truth until you go out and do it, until it has "motor effects" and becomes the tissue and fibre of a good life.

I come next to the Quaker basis of authority in religion. The Quakers have always felt the weakness of tradition or antiquity as a basis of authority. A thing is not necessarily true just because it is hoary with age or because some religious founder in earlier centuries thought it was true and said it was true. The dim magnificence of the halo of tradition may very well impart a beauty and a touch of glory to an idea, but it does not make it true. Nothing is easier than to carry a tradition, or a view, when once it has been launched and given the support of a person of great prestige. But a thousand years of uncontradicted affirmation is unavailing to transform an error into a truth; assertion and repetition are poor substitutes for verification.

Our generation, with its scientific achievements, has learned to have unlimited respect for the authority of facts. It asks for evidence, and evidence again means facts. What does the test-tube say? What does the microscope report? What light does the telescope, or the spectroscope, throw on the topic under discussion? When the laboratory returns are all in and are all summed up, they constitute a powerful authority. The professor who can back up every word with experimental data carries great conviction and speaks as one having authority. The Quaker endeavors to apply that laboratory method to matters of religion. He asks always for the testimony and verification of experience. The historical statements of the Bible, like any other statements, must be tested out by the canons of historical research. No important spiritual truth can suffer by the most careful and honest scrutiny of its historical setting. But the truths themselves, in so far as they have to do with man's spiritual development and destiny, can be tested out best in the laboratory of man's own soul and in the experiences of his own life. "Paul and Silas went to Philippi," is a statement of historical fact, to be tested and verified by the historical method. But the declaration that "the pure in heart see God," can be verified only by inward experimental test. The way to find out whether that is true is not to consult a commentary, or to take counsel with an authoritative priest, but to purify the heart and see what result follows! Religious truth is entirely of that type and nature. It is not up in the air; it is not on stilts; it is not something to be hedged around with tradition and pious phraseology. It is demonstrable and efficacious. It *works* as practically and constructively as electricity does. There is nothing essential to salvation or to the spiritual life of man which cannot be proved and verified as effectively as the facts of the light-spectrum are verified.

Well, in an age in which multitudes have been upset and thrown into doubt and difficulty as to how the realities of religion can be preserved in the face of the revolutionary conclusions of science and historical criticism, I am happy to belong to a little body of Christians who are convinced that the foundations of faith stand sure because they are built upon the eternal nature of the human soul itself, because the most important facts of religion are facts of experience, and finally because everything that has spiritual significance can be tested and verified in the life of man as he lives in relation to God and in relation to his fellow men.

This is what may be called a religion of life, or, equally well, a religion of the spirit. To be religious is to be an organ of the divine Spirit. It means and involves a sensitiveness to the wider spiritual Life above us, around us, and within us, a dedication to duty, a passion for truth, an appreciation for goodness, an eagerness to let the love and grace of God come freely through one's own life, a reverence for the will of God wherever it is revealed in past or present, and a high faith that Christ is a living presence and a life-giving energy always within reach of the receptive soul.

This account, of course, leaves on one side much which many Christians, including many Friends, would consider very important. I do not underestimate the value of those aspects which I have failed to notice. I am here, however, touching only the points which stand out as essential features of the Quaker way of life. Problems of theology, organization, discipline, system, and procedure are not negligible matters, but they can be passed over here without discussion, for I am simply engaged in telling why I choose to be a Friend, and the answer is: because I find among my fellow Friends a religion which is a real, true, vital way of life, and, best of all, I believe a way closely modeled after the Galilean way of the Gospel.

THE SOCIETY OF FRIENDS

THE Society of Friends which sprang up in England in the middle of the seventeenth century is unique among religious denominations in that it has no priest-

hood, liturgy, creed, or sacraments. George Fox, the founder, opposing the two then widely accepted tenets of closed inspiration and authoritative priesthood, proclaimed that God speaks directly to each human soul through a present living experience of Christ,—this inward Light requiring no human mediator to translate its meaning to the individual. The first followers of Fox had no thought of founding a church but were simply known as Children of the Light. Later, when the need for some organization became evident, Fox was active in helping to organize the system of monthly, quarterly, and yearly meetings and in arranging methods of procedure which still obtain.

The method of coming to a decision in these business meetings is democratic. From the beginning women have had equal voice with men. No vote is ever taken. The "sense of the meeting" as revealed by the speakers is registered by the clerk and submitted by him for immediate approval or criticism. Although this method sometimes necessitates delay, in the main it has been found effective.

If worship is the right hand, then social justice is the left hand of Quakerism. Friends have been pioneers in work for the abolition of slavery, for peace, the equality of men and women, education, fair treatment of Indians, temperance, and prison reform.

The approximate membership in the Society of Friends is 146,500 of whom about 23,000 are in Great Britain and Ireland, and 10,000 in other foreign countries. The 113,500 American Friends are distributed among twenty-nine Yearly Meetings.

The Five Years' Meeting and the Friends' General Conference, each composed of a number of separate

Yearly Meetings, have an advisory but no legislative function.

Friends in America have shown a wide variety of observance, from the very conservative meetings in the east to the pastoral system in the west, but of recent years there has been a tendency toward greater unity.

Educational institutions under the care of Friends in the United States include the following colleges: Haverford, Swarthmore, Bryn Mawr, Earlham, Guilford, Penn, Wilmington, Friends University, Pacific, Whittier, and Nebraska Central; a number of boarding schools, of which Moses Brown, Westtown, George School, and Oakwood Seminary are perhaps the best known; and many day schools, most of which are under the care of Monthly Meetings. Several schools for the education of colored people and Indians are maintained. Woolman School is conducted for social and religious study. Missions have been established in Palestine, China, Japan, India, Africa, the West Indies, and Mexico.

The outstanding work sponsored by Friends in recent years has been done through the service committees. The American Friends' Service Committee represents all Friends in America and coöperates in foreign work with English and Irish Friends. Peace work in the home field and active relief, reconstruction, and peace work in the war stricken countries of Europe have called for the volunteer service in America of over a thousand workers and an expenditure of $25,000,000 in cash and kind.

CHAPTER VII

WHY I AM A METHODIST

By

FRANK MASON NORTH

Society of Methodist Missions Board

SOME college societies speak of "born men." They are the sons of former members. There is nothing gained by ignoring the fact that I was a "born" Methodist. Where heredity and environment reach an agreement the decision is apt to be final. There were Methodist history and tradition for two generations of ancestry on the one side, and on the other undisguised and active loyalty. When, at the age of eight, I made for my boy-self experiment of repentance for sin of which I felt personal guilt, and of faith in Jesus Christ as Saviour, in the way which had been from earliest childhood taught me, it would have been strange, had I not stepped through the church door which opened just before me. It is easy to see how I went into the Methodist Episcopal Church. I was reared at its threshold, and the doorsill was low enough for even a little fellow to step over.

But the question is not why I became a Methodist, but why I remained so; why I *am* a Methodist. The query put in this form is seen to be entirely pertinent when one recalls the large number of persons in the membership and the ministry of the other denominations who on suitable occasion will say, "Yes, I was myself once a Methodist." Of course, one admits that a brick once built into a wall, especially if the wall be broad and strong, finds it difficult to dislodge itself.

My earlier impressions of religious activity were not derived wholly from Methodist sources. It is in my boyhood recollection that interests outside the Church commanded the time and thoughts of those who most influenced me. New York was my birthplace and has been my home, or, as foreign missionary folk would say, my home base, for my entire life. The names of several of the existing philanthropic institutions of the city were with us household words in the days of their beginning. It was a Methodist environment, but into it came interests galore that bore other labels or no labels at all.

This study forces retrospect. It is matter of profound gratitude as I look around and look back that almost uniformly the men of other Christian groups whom I have met have given the finest possible expression of the spirit and thought of the special fellowships they have represented. Two warm friends were found in the pastors of the two churches, in the little town of the earliest years of my ministry, the one a Baptist, the other a Presbyterian. Through the one I became familiar with Rochester Seminary and the Baptist Church, through the other with Princeton Seminary and a large part of the Presbyterian Church. The fact that the one, in his doctrinal moods, called me a pedobaptist, and the other found in me an Arminian or, worse, as he believed, a Pelagian, disturbed neither our equanimity nor our friendship. I have for fifty years looked at two great denominations through Alonzo Parker and Will R. Terrett. And this early experience has been but the beginning of the personal contacts which, increasing in the interdenominational activities of the later years, have brought into friendship and fellowship the many men who have ever put into focus the very best things in the thought and action of the churches of which they have been conspicuous representatives.

And yet I am a Methodist. What began with me as a life is confirmed by the logic of experience and observation of the years. When I record what as a Methodist I see in the Church of which I am a member and a minister, I make not the slightest intimation that others must see it as I do, or that the same excellence, if it be such, does not exist in other churches. The fact that I state why I am a Methodist and am content to be one, is neither an argument nor an apology. In old-time Methodist fashion, I simply give my experience.

Begin at the beginning. Baptized as a child in recognition of my part in the redemption brought us by our Lord Jesus Christ, trained and spiritually stimulated by the teaching and example in both church and home, as soon as I could apprehend, even in child fashion, the significance of the "good news" for me, my personal relation to the church was solemnly defined and I became consciously a part of it. The other course would have been for me to have heard the truth through the years of late childhood and adolescence, remaining outside the church family and excluded from the sacraments which appeal so strongly to the mobile minds of the young, and at some time have been arrested by conscience or circumstance, or both, and then through repentance for sins which perchance otherwise never would have been committed, and confession of faith, formally to accept membership in the church. Methodism has from the beginning been hospitable to the child. In her theology she finds for the little ones a warm place by the fireside. Her vigorous promotion of the Sunday School and its positive evangelism, her emphasis upon home religion, upon family prayer, upon the duty of parents, her persistent study of the child in his relation to the church, and her adjustment of method and plan to bring to the children of the church the requisite preparation for intelligent membership therein, are indications of her conviction as to the right of childhood in the Gospel. In the last official statement we read: "We hold that all children, by virtue of the unconditional benefits of the atonement, are members of the Kingdom of God, and, therefore, graciously entitled to baptism; but, as infant baptism contemplates a course of religious instruction and discipline, it is expected of all parents or guardians who present their children for baptism that they will use all diligence in bringing them up in conformity to the word of God; and they should be solemnly admonished of this obligation and earnestly exhorted to faithfulness therein. We regard all children who have been baptized as placed in visible covenant relation to God and as preparatory members under the special care and supervision of the Church." Here is no attempt to describe the ministries of the Methodist Church to children, in its vast range of Sunday Schools, its Junior Epworth Leagues, its missionary organizations, its orphanages, its homes; rather, only, to mark the significance of the essential conviction as to the relation of the child to the Kingdom of God and to the Church and to offer this as one of the reasons why I am content to be a Methodist. I like a church which deals with the child not as alien, but as one of the family.

In the matter of the Christian ministry much that is irrelevant is driven out of the mind of one who is accepting it as a lifework, if one is moved by an inner persuasion which can be accepted as God's mandate. With one's mind cleared of doubt one looks out upon one's lifework with a sort of impartial curiosity. Two phases of that life confronted me as, in a rather detached way, I looked at it, having accepted the mandate. The one had to do with the message, the other with the method. In both ranges the facts have seemed to me to conform to my earlier forecast of them.

The message was and is "good news,"—the very best news that came to the world. The ruling motive, as I conceived it, was not its protection, but its circulation. The best minds could exhaust their powers in communicating it, but even simple and untrained souls could pass it on. The news was for everybody. Redemption moved in the great circles. It was not limited to a small group of saints within the great circle of humanity, nor to a segment of the great circle. All men everywhere are to hear the news and to have the opportunity to repent. And where the news comes to them and they are moved to accept Christ, and to put their trust in Him, they need not be told that by some immutable and eternal decree of an all-wise God they

may possibly not have been included in the
number of the elect. Both in England and
America and now in every land the message
which it has been and is the privilege of the
Church to give to the multitudes is that which
was rather quaintly called "a free and a full
salvation," dependent for its effectiveness
upon the will of the individual to surrender
to its conditions and to accept its resources,—
a will ever reënforced by the power of the
Divine Spirit.

In these days no one hesitates to accept the
high values in both Calvinism and Arminian-
ism. They are two phases of one unshaken
truth. The schools,—some of them,—still rejoice in the controversies which they en-
gender. The message which is winning the
world has place for the sovereignty of God,
but its working basis is in the fact that "God
so loved the world that He gave His only be-
gotten Son that whosoever believeth in Him
might not perish but have everlasting life."
Whatever else it did or did not do, the "Wesleyan Revival" and the organized work which
came out of it found in John 3:16 the magnet
to which all other scattered beliefs were
drawn. Central in its history and in the pres-

ent program of Methodism, the "whosoever" doctrine holds me to the Methodist Church. I believe in the message. Its warmth opens its way. It wins in the realm of the heart. It deals with men as they are, without waiting to explain how they got there. It stands the test as a revelation of the character of God and a disclosure of the desperate need of the human spirit.

It is with the message in mind that one finds the interpretation of the work of the early Methodist itinerants. The circuit rider has got into our American history, and, for aught one can see, must stay there. The Asbury Statue in Washington is more than a Church's memorial, it is a symbol and calls to the nation's attention those traveling heroes who, as was true of the first bearers of the message, "went through the land preaching the Gospel." The early Wesleyan preachers in America, with the exception of Francis Asbury, their leader by assignment and personal qualities, returned to England during the Revolution, but they could not take away from their American fellows the message. During the struggle and in the years thereafter, these itinerants were a mighty conservative and creative force. The historians have not over-looked them. For the most part, they were not scholars, but they had brains. They were keen debaters. They were patient and fear-less. Their hearts were aflame. Their mes-sage was fused in the fire of their own experience. In one sense it was a "settled" ministry. They were settled in the saddle. A competent and judicial historian writes of them:

Chivalry, romance unsurpassed in modern history, at least since the days of the Crusades, color all their experi-ences. Absorbed as they were in the value of the individ-ual soul, their imaginations were not kindled by any dreams of ecclesiastical empire. Pictures of modern Methodist edifices or of modern Methodist audiences could have yielded them no inspiration. They believed and therefore they spoke. They had souls to take care of, and they cared for them in the best methods which their intellects could devise. Leaving to God the business of opening doors, and accepting for themselves the humbler business of entering such doors as He might open enabled the Methodist pioneers, as it enables all the elect of God, to do a work of whose importance and magnitude the farthest-sighted of them all had only faint and uncertain glimpses.

Theodore Roosevelt once paid tribute to these heroic men in words worth record here:

We were a nation of pioneers. In the hard and cruel life of the border there was much to pull the frontiersman down. If left to himself without moral teaching and moral guidance . . . sad would have been his, and, therefore, our fate. From this fate we have been largely rescued by the fact that together with the rest of the pioneers went the pioneer preachers; and all honor be to Methodism for the large proportion of those pioneer preachers which it furnished. These preachers were men . . . who suffered and overcame every hardship in common with their flock, and who, in common with their flock, endured. That is the kind of leadership that counts. And, in addition, they tamed the wild and fierce spirit of their fellow pioneers. . . . (They) warred against the forces of spiritual evil with the same fiery zeal and energy that they and their fellows showed in the conquest of a rugged continent. They had in them the heroic spirit, the spirit that scorns ease if it must be purchased by failure to do duty, the spirit that courts risk and a life of hard endeavor if the goal to be reached is really worth attaining. Great is our debt to these men and scant the patience we need show toward their critics.

When I consider these men, I count myself unworthy of their fellowship, but happy indeed, if I may, to belong to it.

One must still consider the message if the worldwide expansion of Methodism is to be understood. Wesley gave his followers doctrines, it is true, but chiefly he gave them a spirit and a method. As to range he fixed no limit. It is probably not known just how much he meant when he said, "The world is my parish," but his successors have found no difficulty in the interpretation. His organization was not a church, but a movement. Crystallization into statement and form has been inevitable, but Methodism is a stream, not an inland sea. It does not simply reflect the skies and lap the pebbly beaches of its own shores, but it find channels, or makes them, into other climates and out upon other levels. This is characteristic of the missionary purpose in all churches. The point here made is that it was essential in Methodism from the beginning and is in it an incurable trait.

One of my early Christian duties was to be the collector and treasurer for missionary funds for the Sunday School class of which I was a member, the humble name we bore being "Dewdrops," and the monthly accumulation of the silvery refreshment indicated was three silver dollars. The Sunday Schools of the Church were organized into Sunday School Missionary Societies. The general society was the Missionary Society of the Methodist Episcopal Church. It was established in 1819, the third of the great American Societies in order, being preceded by The American Board of Commissions for Foreign Missions (1810), and the General Convention of the Baptist Denomination in the United States of America for Foreign Missions (1814). The unhappy division of the Methodist Episcopal Church in 1844 required a new Society for the Southern part of the Church, but the division lessened neither the ardor nor the output. Recently the Missionary Centenary has been celebrated by both bodies, and surveys of the worldwide work are accessible. The slogans, the goals, the denominational achievements, the zeal of these ten decades of Methodist missionary work have been under review from every angle. The Church starts into its second Missionary Centenary with the conviction that it is its business to do its part to see that no man anywhere, in our favored homeland or in the remotest corner of the globe, is denied his chance to hear and to understand the message of the Gospel. This is the real interpretation of that consuming zeal, sometimes miscalled a sectarian spirit, which is found in the thousands of devoted men and women who

have been building themselves into the new
world fabric and of the tens of millions of
dollars which, however inadequate to the
need, have been a glad contribution toward
getting the world to hear and understand the
"good news!" A church which hesitates at
no threshold where the Gospel is needed, and
offers itself for service wherever the people
are, appeals both to my enthusiasm and my
confidence.

There is much more to be said about the
message, but we must come to the matter of
method. Here at once I am challenged
with the query how, being rather keen myself about individual freedom, I can endure being tied up in a hierarchy, how being
of a democratic spirit I can be content to
work in even a well articulated organization
which I cannot control. Well, one cannot in
a few words tell the whole story, but parts of
it belong here. The Church means not only
a testimony, but a program. The history of
the development of the Wesleyan Church in
England and of the Methodist Episcopal
Church in America and in the rest of the
world is an ecclesiastical romance. Here is a
record of the development of form from the

inner spirit as circumstances and reason required. Essentially the movement was a matter of life,—but since life means conduct, rules
and method soon followed and grew into a
system of action. Certainly the Methodist
Church,—I refer now to the two larger
branches known as the Methodist Episcopal
Church,—is not a pure democracy. Just as
surely it is not an autocracy. The ministry
is made by the people. No man secures orders
except by the suffrage of those who with him
are first licensed by the laity to preach and
are by the Church through its proper agency,
—District or Quarterly Conference,—recom-
mended for the ministry. Bishops have certain authority,—authority which can be, but
rarely is, misused. They do not constitute a
third order in the ministry. They are not
"prelates." They are general superintendents
with duties of oversight, restricted powers,
and extraordinary opportunity for personal
leadership. Their administration is in every
fourth year, at the General Conference, re-
viewed. The body which elects them and
reviews their official conduct is itself as representative as is possible in a great organization.
Within the Church, in its largest sense, is pro-

vision for organization for specific ends. The mechanism is sometimes faulty, occasionally "static" interferes. But extraordinary provision is made, in carefully articulated groups, for the promotion of woman's work, of Sunday schools, of education, of home missions, of reform, of philanthrophies, of social service, of foreign missions, of coöperation with other churches; in a word the method shaped by the invention and the attrition of the years lends itself continually to such use and adaptation as, in the main, finds for the message its way of expression to the strangely assorted groups which together form what we call the world.

Within this organization there is freedom. Order is essential to smooth operation. One may think without embarrassment. There are, it is true, essentials of belief with which every thinker, while a Methodist, reckons. They are the very essence of the faith. They are tested by twenty centuries and belong to the Church universal. They are held to be Biblical,—theology which squares with revelation and experience and which works. There are, of course, many marginal notes, but they have been kept out of the text.

Methodism has bones as well as arteries and
nerves. There is a frame as well as circulation and feeling. In his famous tract on "The
Character of a Methodist," John Wesley
wrote:

The distinguishing marks of a Methodist are not his
opinions of any sort. His assenting to this or to that
scheme of religion, his embracing of any particular set of
notions, his espousing the judgment of one man or of
another, are all quite wide of the point. Whosoever,
therefore, imagines that a Methodist is a man of such and
such an opinion, is grossly ignorant of the whole affair;
he mistakes the truth totally. We believe, indeed, that
'all Scripture is given by the inspiration of God'; and
herein we are distinguished from Jews, Turks, and Infi-
dels. We believe the written word of God to be the only
and sufficient rule both of Christian faith and practice;
and herein we are fundamentally distinguished from those
of the Romish Church. We believe Christ to be the
eternal, supreme God; and herein we are distinguished
from the Socinians and Arians. But as to all opinions
which do not strike at the root of Christianity, we think
and let think. So that whatsoever they are, whether right
or wrong, they are no distinguishing marks of a Methodist.

When Mr. Wesley prepared a doctrinal
basis for the Methodist Societies in America
by revising and reducing the Thirty-nine Ar-

ticles of The Church of England, he exercised a freedom with those articles which is at once an illustration of his freehand dealing with the archaic and a proof of his good sense in interpreting what a new church in a new land might not require. He transferred, however, with practically no change, the article "Of the sufficiency of the Holy Scriptures for Salvation," as follows: "The Holy Scriptures contain all things necessary to salvation so that whatsoever is not read therein, nor may be proved thereby, is not to be required of any man that it should be believed as an article of faith, or be thought requisite or necessary to salvation." The Holy Office can hardly be invoked under these terms. The rack and the thumbscrew belong in the museums. As a matter of fact we suspect that most Methodists are both fundamentalist and modernist. They are less interested in the tiltyard of controversy, than in the broad highway of service. They observe with interest the present virulent epidemic of intolerance. The liberals have it in as dangerous a form as the standpatters. The Methodist Church is largely, though not entirely, free from the infection. May its general health and such

mild inoculations as it has already had keep it
free from the poison that is in the air.

Of other reasons why it contents me to remain a Methodist there can be here but brief-
est mention. They may be summarized.

The Methodist interest in education. Here
is a story which reaches from the early attempts to establish "Ebenezer" Academy in
Virginia, 1760-64, and Cokesbury College in
Maryland (1787), through the efforts, wherever the Church became stable, to create
academies and later colleges until at this writing there exist in this country thirty-six
secondary schools, fifty-five colleges and uni-
versities, and forty-four professional schools.
Out of the fertile mind of a Methodist leader
came the Chautauqua idea and plan, an educational influence for the common people the
range of which can hardly be overstated. The
Church holds that education is an evangelistic
force, as witness its schools in the South and
on the frontier and in all its mission fields.
Its theory of education at home and abroad is
that, while its schools may provide under religious auspices for the children of the
Church, the doors should swing wide for all
others. It unfailingly supports the public

schools system. Its ideal of freedom finds illustration in the terms of the first charter of Wesleyan University, Middletown, Connecticut, established in 1831. The charter includes the following: "Provided, that no by-law or ordinances shall be established by said corporation, which shall make the religious tenets of any person a condition of admission to any privilege in said University; and that no president, professor, or other officer shall be made ineligible for or by reason of any religious tenets that he may profess nor be compelled, by any by-laws or otherwise, to subscribe to any religious test whatever." This is an illustration, not a universal rule. It indicates, however, the broad, non-sectarian spirit of the church's educational program.

The Methodist conviction as to the position of women in the Church. The mother of the Wesleys is revered as one of the ablest of English women and one of the noblest of Christians. The work of women in the church has always been encouraged and in the development of the church's polity has been officially recognized. The offices in the local church have practically always been open to her. She has membership in the General

[145]

Conference. She has control of most important interests in organized Boards for woman's work and is increasingly welcomed upon the General Boards. She is eligible to ordination as a local preacher, though not admitted to Conference membership and appointment as such to a pastorate. It is interesting to note that the Protestant Episcopal Church and the Methodist Episcopal Church both derived their marriage ritual from the Church of England, and that, while the former is just now agitated in the matter of omitting from the vow taken by the woman the word "obey," the latter made the change over sixty years ago.

The Methodist attitude toward reform. The Church divided in 1844 on the question of holding slaves. The withdrawal of the churches of the South was an honorable procedure. The moral conviction of the major portion of the Church was not shaken by what seemed a catastrophe. Twenty years later the slaves were freed. To the freed slaves the Church gave her help, to the freed owners the Church held out her hand. Unafraid, the original Church, larger by far than any of its branches, bore through troublous years her testimony against human slavery. As this is written, her Conferences, clerical and lay, are voting with practical unanimity for the plan which would heal the breach made eighty years ago.

In statute and in practice, the Methodist Episcopal Church has been for a century a total abstinence church. It has taught the principle to its children, it has been potently active in every organized effort to drive out the saloon, to save the home from the woe of intemperance, to put prohibitory laws upon the statute books of States and nation, and now it works unceasingly for the enforcement of law.

Methodism has been sensitive to the disasters, the distress, the injustices, and the inequities of the social and industrial order. In spirit and in action it has been from its beginning the friend of the poor. It was early a city missionary and its members were familiar among the saving forces in the dark places of the cities. It went into the Five Points, for example, as far back as 1849. In New York it definitely organized a city missionary Society in 1862. The General Conference of 1908 approved The Methodist Federation for

Social Service and adopted a series of statements, remarkable for the time, in the interest
of justice in industry which, in part, embodied
in the action of The Federal Council of
Churches that same year, contributed substantially to the social creed of the churches
widely adopted by our American denominations. Not in every respect, nor in every one
of its agencies has the church given its witness
for necessary changes in the social order, but
Methodism is of the people, in them is its life,
for them it will give itself ever more justly
and generously.

Methodists have believed in the nation and,
as citizens and as soldiers, they have served it.
The testimony of three wars gives them no
uncertain place in the ranks of those who have
defended the rights of the people or have
fought to redress their wrongs. If this were
all, one could not be content. This, numer-
ically the largest Protestant Church in America, with vision and conviction as to its world
task, is stirring itself for the international
duties which the form of its worldwide organization and the essentials of its message
demand. Should its spirit cool while its opportunities broaden it would itself lose,—the

world would lose. But it has failures enough for wholesome humiliation and self-discipline, and it is eager to meet the new day. It is warmed by the zeal of its companions in the great onward movement, it is strengthened by their might, it is comforted by their fellowship. They have elements of attraction and of force which would enrich Methodism, and, it is not unlikely, add to its effectiveness.

But the history, the essential doctrines, the ideals, the worldwideness, the fellowship, the adaptiveness, the glow, the courage, and the efficiency,—in a word, the message and the method of the Methodist Episcopal Church hold me both in conviction and in service.

METHODISM

A LL the fifteen branches of Methodism in the United *States have come from the one stem. The evangelical revival in Great Britain in the eighteenth century reached America in the hearts of the emigrant members of the societies organized by John Wesley. He, his brother Charles, and George Whitefield were, humanly speaking, the inspirers, the leaders, and the embodiment of the movement.*

[149]

TWELVE MODERN APOSTLES

By the latest authoritative statement the Methodist group within the United States shows a membership of 8,920,190. In this total five units account for 8,580,948. Of these, two major bodies, The Methodist Episcopal Church and The Methodist Episcopal Church, South, have in membership 7,050,918; the other three are colored churches, numbering 1,530,030. Ten bodies together have 339,242 members. If to its membership in the United States that in foreign lands is added approximately 630,000, the total for the Methodist group would be 9,550,190.

The sequence of events gives the history in epitome: 1766, the first British Wesleyan Society in New York; 1769, Boardman and Pilmoor sent over by John Wesley as missionaries; 1771, Richard Wright and Francis Asbury appointed to America; 1773 (July 14) the first Methodist "Conference" in America; 1784, Thomas Coke ordained by Wesley with commission to ordain Francis Asbury, appointing them "joint Superintendents over our Brethren in America"; 1784 (December 24) the "Christmas" Conference in Baltimore, Coke and Asbury (the latter refusing appointment without election) elected Superintendents, and Asbury consecrated Superintendent by Coke, in pursuance of Wesley's authorization and election by the Conference: Adoption by this Conference of the first "Discipline of The Methodist Episcopal Church", including Constitution and Ritual; 1812, First Delegated General Conference; 1816, Organization of the African Methodist Episcopal Church; 1844-5 withdrawal of The Methodist Episcopal Church, South.

In organization The Methodist Episcopal Church has

for its legislative governing body The General Conference, which meets quadrennially, and is composed in equal numbers of lay and ministerial members; for working units the Annual Conferences of which all ministers and they only, are members; The General Boards,—Foreign Missions, Home Missions, Education, Temperance and Reform, Hospitals and Homes, Pensions; for superintendence, the Bishops, with power to select as advisers, district superintendents, to assign pastors to churches, and, in general to supervise the work of the church, with special responsibility for that in the Conferences in the Areas to which they are assigned by the General Conference for residence.

The Methodist Episcopal Church has a registration of over 5,000,000 scholars and teachers in its Sunday schools and over 725,000 members in its Young Peoples Society (Epworth League). It has 30,000 churches and nearly 20,000 ministers. Its Publishing House (The Methodist Book Concern) by recent report shows sales for the last year of over $5,000,000, and a capital of $6,588-000. It has 78 hospitals under its auspices, providing over 7,300 beds, and representing property and endowment of more than $30,000,000. Its Homes for The Aged number forty, with a capacity for nearly 2,000. It maintains forty-five Homes for Children, with a capacity of about 3,000.

Chapter VIII

WHY I AM
A CONGREGATIONALIST

By

Charles Edward Jefferson
Pastor of The Broadway Tabernacle

SOME are born Congregationalists, and some have Congregationalism thrust upon them, but by my own efforts I achieved my place in the Congregational Church. My parents were not Congregationalists, nor were my grandparents, nor my great-grandparents. There was not a Puritan in my ancestry for ten generations. I was born in the Middle West where Congregationalists were unknown, and I was over twenty years of age before I saw a live Congregationalist. At sixteen I joined the church of my parents, and there I might have remained to this day had I not at the age of twenty-four decided to enter the ministry. Having resolved to become a minister, the question as to what de-

WHY I AM A CONGREGATIONALIST

nomination I could do my best work in came at once to the front. I pondered the problem for three years, and finally decided to become a Congregationalist. I have preached in Congregationalist pulpits for nearly forty years, and have never once in all that time regretted my choice. If I were permitted to come back to the earth in a new incarnation, I should ask for a place among the Congregationalists.

It was the freedom which Congregationalism offers which won me. I was born with a passionate love of liberty. Freedom of thought was always to me one of the most sacred of all human rights. Anything like coercion in the realm of religion was to me especially abhorrent. I did not take kindly to the idea of ecclesiastical dictation. I would never have made a happy monk. The vow of absolute and unquestioning obedience to any human being would have been impossible. I studied the history and polity of all the denominations, and found that Congregationalism offers the largest liberty while retaining all the beliefs and traditions which I considered essential to a vital and conquering church.

The Baptists are Congregationalists in church government, but they insist on immersion as the only valid form of baptism. They also deny the right of Christian parents to have their children baptized into the name of Christ. This insistence on one particular form of baptism seemed to me entirely foreign to the genius of the religion of Jesus, and I could not identify myself with a body of Christian people who would not admit into their ecclesiastical fellowship any Christian who had not been immersed. Congregationalism is not interested in forms. It accepts the sacrament of baptism, but the form of baptism it considers immaterial. It always stresses the spiritual rather than the formal, and refuses to make any ceremony a cardinal feature of the Christian religion. It does not insist on Christian parents having their children baptized, for it recognized the force of the arguments which can be brought against that practice, and it is not willing that parents should be coerced to follow a custom which does not commend itself to their judgment. On the other hand it refuses to deny baptism to little children. The baptism of infants has been practised among the majority of Christians from very early times, and a custom in whose favor so much can be said, and which is so satisfying and precious to multitudes of hearts, is one which Congregationalists are not willing to cast out. Freedom here, as in other matters, is the Congregational doctrine. One reason why I am a Congregationalist instead of a Baptist is because I agree with the Congregational position on baptism.

Presbyterianism is closely related to Congregationalism in various ways. The two denominations have constantly influenced and modified each other. In temperament and in general type of character Congregationalists are more like Presbyterians than any other body of Christians. While the forms of government are different, Presbyterianism allows large liberties to its adherents, and doctrinally the two denominations were for two hundred years practically one. Both were strongly Calvinistic, and their general interpretation of the Bible was substantially the same. But I could not become a Presbyterian because I did not like the Westminster Confession, and I was not willing to subscribe to it even in the loose way which has become common and which is defended by learned and conscientious men. I was not a Calvinist and I was not inclined to put my head in the Calvinistic yoke. Moreover I was afraid of the General Assembly. It possessed, it seemed to me, too much power. I feared that at times I might be compelled to be a rebel. I wanted larger liberty than Presbyterianism was able to offer. I found it in Congregationalism. The autonomy of the local church is fundamental with us. We take our name from this principle. We are ruled not by Popes or by Bishops or by General Councils, but by the Congregation. We are Congregation-ists. There is no ecclesiastical authority above the local congregation. The local congregation is free to elect its own officers, choose its own Pastors, adopt its own form of worship, formulate its own creed, and frame its own program. It is a free church. A Congregational Pastor cannot be dictated to by any one outside his church. There is no ecclesiastical tribunal or legislature or court to which he must bow. He and his congregation are left unshackled to work out their own salvation. If a Congregational Church does not prosper, it is not due to any ill-advised interference from without, but solely from lack of spiritual wisdom and vitality in the Pastor and his people.

Each Congregational Church answers directly to God for the use it makes of its talents. To be sure, we have our Councils and conferences and associations, but these are not endowed with authority over the local congregation. Congregationalists do not believe in isolation. They know that isolation is death. They believe in fellowship and in coöperation. They believe in the sisterhood of the churches. They know that the churches are comrades in a great campaign, coworkers in a vast and difficult enterprise. And so our churches help one another. They band themselves together to forward noble causes. They meet at stated times in regional and national councils, to confer together about their common work. These councils are not courts or legislatures. They enact no laws. They hand down no judicial decisions. All their declarations are advisory. They are to be taken for what they are worth. Their worth is determined by the people in our congregations. Congregationalists do not consider any resolutions or recommendations passed by church councils as binding on themselves, unless their

own conscience can give its approval. Our
ecclesiastical bodies give advice only. They
can express the judgment of a group of representatives of the churches, but they cannot
compel action. There is no legal coercion in
our denomination. When we do things it is
not because we have been ordered to do them
by some ecclesiastical tribunal, but because
the love of Christ constrains us. Our churches
are bound together not by legal enactments,
but by the Spirit. We have no Cardinals or
Bishops to whip us into line. We rely solely
on the guidance of the Spirit. A theorist
might suppose we would fall into chaos, but
we do not. We have tried this experiment
over three hundred years, and we have never
fallen into chaos yet. We are quite compact
and wonderfully united.

A spirit of unity not surpassed in any other
Communion runs through the entire Congregational denomination. We have no creed
which is binding on our people. We use
creeds not as tests but as testimony. In our
creeds we bear witness to the truths which we
as a body of Christian men and women believe. Any one can join one of our churches
simply by confessing allegiance to Jesus

Christ as Lord and Saviour. Our National Council has laid before the churches a creed formulated by a committee of devout and able clergymen and laymen, but this creed is not binding. Some of our churches use it, others do not. Some of our churches prefer the Apostles' Creed, others have no written creed at all. Creed subscription cuts no figure with us. We know nothing of "mental reservations." We are not compelled to explain to heresy hunting committees just what we mean. We are free. We are at liberty to follow the Truth wherever the Truth may lead us. No pressure is put on the individual intellect. The conscience is not subjected to coercion. We trust wholly to the Spirit. The founder of Christianity assured His disciples that the Holy Spirit would guide them into all truth, and we accept that promise with confidence and act upon it boldly. I am not a Presbyterian because I want a wider liberty than Presbyterianism is willing to allow.

I might have entered the Episcopal Church had that church allowed more liberty in the order of its worship. The prayer book is a precious inheritance, and deserves to be prized highly. It belongs to the whole church of Christ, and all Christians should use it so far as they can get help from it. But I could not accept the prayer book as it stands. There are some things in it I dislike, and a few things which I abhor. It has beauties, but it also has its imperfections and limitations. Its chief defect, in my judgment, is that it binds too closely the actions of the local congregations. There is no reason why all the congregations in a large country like ours should worship God every Sunday morning in the same form of words. Different localities present different needs, and different classes of people demand different forms. What is helpful to some is irksome to others. Worship when imposed from without is in danger of becoming a burden and a bore. I like the Congregational freedom better. A Congregational Church is at liberty to worship God in its own way. This is a privilege which belongs to every group of believers. Each church should, it seems to me, be allowed to adopt whatever forms of worship are best adapted to build up the spiritual life of the people. Moreover, I could not go into the Episcopal Church because it helps to keep alive the mischievous fiction of Apostolic Succession, one of the most demoralizing of all the superstitions which have afflicted the Church of Christ. Nothing is more foreign to the spirit of Congregationalism than this mechanical theory of clerical orders. Congregationalists do not believe that the new Testament prescribes any one form of church government, or that Jesus of Nazareth ever gave any instructions either before or after his death in regard to the grades and authority of church officials. The only successors of the Apostles, according to our way of thinking, are men who have the spirit and do the work of the Apostles. This is the teaching of Congregationalism, and in this I steadfastly believe.

I love Congregationalism because of its breadth. It is not sectarian in temper or policy. It is not exclusive or snobbish. It does not claim that it is the only true church. It holds that all churches are true churches which have the Spirit of Christ. It does not maintain that its government is the only divinely appointed government. It concedes that all governments are allowable which Christian men are able to make use of to the glory of God. It does not claim that its gov-

ernment is the best government. All it claims
is that it is a good form of government, and
that it is capable of being used in the advancement of the kingdom of truth and justice and
love. Congregationalists do not attempt to
push their polity upon others. This is why
our Communion is small. It has not mattered
to our leaders what church polity is made use
of. Their supreme concern has been with the
promulgation of Christian principles and the
building up of Christian character.

I am proud of my denomination because of
its trust in the people. It has supreme confidence in the common man. It believes in
Democracy both in Church and in State.
Congregationalism is Democracy in religion.
Since all men are children of God and open
to the Spirit of God, all men who have sur-
rendered to Christ can be trusted with the
responsibility of shaping the policy of the
Church of Christ. This is the conviction of
Congregationalism. I am proud of it because of its catholicity of spirit. We believe
in the Holy Catholic Church, and by Catholic
we mean universal. We call all Christians,—
Catholics and Protestants of every name, and

[162]

with all denominations we are ready to work at all times for the building up of men in love.

I am proud of our history and of the invaluable contribution we have made to human progress. We have gloried in liberty and have striven mightily to establish it in the world. We have exalted the reason and have built colleges all over the land. We have had the world vision and in our missionary enterprises we have been in the forefront of those eager to conquer the world for Christ. We are a small regiment, but we are valiant fighters. We do not make much noise but we are potent. Like leaven we are always at work, and our influence extends to the ends of the earth. We rejoice greatly in the size and enthusiasm and achievements of our sister denominations, the heavy battalions of the Lord's army, and we are thankful that God has given us also a place on the field, and that in more than one critical situation he has allowed us to lead the way.

CONGREGATIONALISM

*THE Congregational Churches of the United States
are a fellowship of some six thousand churches
which are the spiritual descendants of the Pilgrims and
Puritans who first came to America in 1620.*

*The movement out of which these churches came into
being had its rise in the sixteenth century in England,
when many turned from the Established Church in order
to have more independence and simplicity in their religious
life and organization. The various church bodies that
sprang from this movement have many common characteristics, among these are the love for democratic forms
of social organization in Church and State, their desire
for education, and their insistence on the primacy of the
Bible as a guide and instructor.*

*The local congregation is a body of believers who are
convened together for religious worship, work, and fellowship, acknowledging Christ as the only authoritative
head. They renounce the right of the state to control
religion, maintain the ideal of a personal experience of
religion for every believer and seek to reproduce the New
Testament ideal of simplicity and democracy.*

*The local congregations have fellowship together in
the Associations, State Conferences, and the National
Council. These organizations are formed by regularly
elected delegates from the churches and church groups.
The ideal of the connectional system is "independence in
individual concern, coöperation in common concern."*

*Congregational Churches emphasize beliefs in which
all evangelical Christians agree, exalt nothing trivial or*

[164]

sectarian, repudiate dogmatism and all legislative control, ecclesiastical or civic, of the spiritual life, and seek union of all churches, on the basis of mutual freedom and fellowship. Their rule of action is "In essentials unity, in non-essentials liberty, in all things charity."

The churches own property to the value of $155,000,-000, an increase of $11,000,000 in the year. The churches raised for current expenses more than $20,000,-000 in 1925, an increase of more than a million dollars over the preceding year. Of this amount $7,602,000 was paid ministers as salaries. The average salary for the year was $1,969, an increase of about $400 over the average salary of five years ago. The gifts to denominational Mission Boards for the year 1925 were $3,179,316, a growth for the year of $66,796, and a growth of over $700,000 in the five-year period.

For the year 1925, the report shows 5,636 churches and a total membership of 901,660. This is a decrease of about 300 churches in the last five years, and an increase of about 80,000 in membership. The decrease in the number of churches with an increase in membership is very significant as it indicates the movement of small churches to merge with nearby Congregational churches or with some other religious body, thus lessening competition in over-churched areas. The growing membership of the churches indicates a vigorous life and a practical program of evangelism which has characterized the denomination in recent years.

The Congregational Churches have pioneered in the promotion of education, missions, evangelism, and in most movements for Christian union, religious progress, and moral reform.

CHAPTER IX

WHY I AM A UNITARIAN
By
SAMUEL MCCHORD CROTHERS
Pastor of First Church, Cambridge

I MAY best begin my answer to the question propounded by the Editor of THE FORUM by quoting from a letter of Charles Lamb to Southey, who had publicly taunted him for forsaking the wholesome forms and doctrines of the Church of England and associating himself with a sect then much spoken against.

Lamb writes: "I am a dissenter; the last sect with which you can remember me to have made common cause were the Unitarians." The reason Lamb gives for this affiliation was a natural affinity rather than agreement in a theological system.

"There are those," he says, "who tremblingly reach out shaking hands to the guidance of faith. There are those who stoutly venture into the dark (their human confidence their leader, which they mistake for faith), and investing themselves with cherubic wings find their new robes as familiar and fitting to their supposed growth and station in godliness as the coat they left off yesterday. Some whose hope totters on crutches—others who stalk into Futurity on stilts. . . . The difference is chiefly constitutional."

I would say that my Unitarianism, such as it is, is chiefly constitutional. It results from the fact that to one of my habit of mind elaborate rituals seem tedious, and formal creeds seem misleading and unnecessary; and the assertion of ecclesiastical authority is irritating. I do not object to the use of crutches, but I do dislike a religion that walks on stilts. I cannot remember when I did not feel so.

I was brought up in the strictest school of the Presbyterians, and while still in my teens was ordained as a Presbyterian minister. My earliest recollections are of a big brick Presbyterian church, which bore a tablet with the inscription, SAMUEL CROTHERS, D.D. My grandfather had organized the church, and continued its minister till his death. He was followed by his son, Samuel, who celebrated the centenary of his father's installation. The oldest inhabitant of the town could not remember the time when Samuel Crothers was not preaching every Sunday in the brick Presbyterian meeting-house. I remember still my resistance to a venerable minister of the Presbytery, when he lifted me into the pulpit and greeted me with pious facetiousness as Samuel the Third. The indignity still rankles.

Presbyterianism was a matter of course, but I never remember to have taken it as anything but as one of the many forms of religion. It happened to be the one within whose fold I was born. In our household intellectual liberty was taken for granted. I learned the Westminster Catechism by heart and received as a reward Moffatt's *Missionary Journeys in South Africa.* But at the same time I read Plutarch's *Lives* and the *Meditations of Marcus Aurelius.*

There was nothing stilted or unnatural in the religion of our household. I never remember to have felt any constraint. I rummaged at will in my grandfather's library and was never warned against dangerous books. There I found the books of the English deists side by side with their orthodox

brethren. There I became acquainted with
Thomas Paine's *Rights of Man.* My grandfather, before he decided to be a minister, had
been the president of a Thomas Paine Club
in a Kentucky college. He always admired
the sturdy radical, though he regretted the
Age of Reason. Theodore Parker had been
an honored name in our Presbyterian family
in the years when conservative Unitarians
looked upon it with distrust. Abolitionism
was a strong tie uniting men of differing theological opinions.

I remember reading a volume of sermons
by my grandmother's brother, James Mc-
Chord, minister of the Market Street Presbyterian Church of Lexington, Kentucky, and
first President of Centre College. There I
got my first introduction to the word "evolution," which now seems so dangerous. The
book was published in 1818, when Darwin
was a small boy. My great-uncle wrote,
"Progressive evolution is the universal plan.
Everything which we meet in the world
around us, matter and mind, every individual
and all congregated masses, begin their
course as germs and unfold in slow progression. . . . The faculties of all intelligent

[169]

creation, all that you call mind, all that you call heart are framed for an interminable series of evolutions. . . . It is not mainly the *mould* of this mighty frame of things which establishes, it is the fact that creation is in an incipient state eternally unfolding new resources and presenting itself under successive and amazing combinations of which no creature in the universe had imagined it capable."

This second Presbyterian doctrine I was glad to find had been confirmed by scientific investigation. So it happened that I grew up as a liberal Presbyterian, and after passing through Princeton and Union Seminary was duly ordained and commissioned by the Board of Home Missions to preach the gospel in Nevada. At my ordination I declared my acceptance of the system of doctrine taught in the Westminster Confession, but I did not at the time feel the necessity of defining what that system was. I determined to preach the truth as I found it, and not cross a bridge till I came to it.

After two or three years, I came to the bridge. For the first time the ethics of creedal conformity gave me trouble. Nobody in the church made any objection to my preaching. I must be my own heresy hunter, but once begun I resolved to make a thorough job of it. I had promised to preach according to the system contained in the Westminster Confession of Faith. Was I doing it? I reread the Confession and found it terrifyingly lucid. These seventeenth century divines had a remarkable skill in defining exactly what they meant.

When I completed my self-imposed task as heresy hunter, there was no reasonable doubt in my mind. Whatever I was preaching, it was not the doctrine which I had promised to preach. So I ceased to be a Presbyterian minister and resolved not to enter the ministry of any church that demanded adherence to any formal creed. The Professor of Chemistry in the university is not asked to subscribe to a chemical creed formulated in a past era. He is required to know his science and to aid in its advancement. He does not forfeit his position because he makes a new discovery. Why should a teacher of religion submit to conditions that render progress impossible and destroy respect for his own intellect? It was not a particular creed that I objected to but the whole creedal system.

One church I found that had definitely put itself on the basis that seemed to me to be sound. In uniting with the Unitarian Church I was not conscious of changing my views, or adopting new doctrines. As a matter of fact, I was preaching very much as I had in a Presbyterian pulpit. But I had got rid of an incumbrance that had become intolerable. I do not care for the Unitarian name any more than Channing or Martineau did. When I read tracts on Unitarian affirmations they kindle in me no sectarian zeal. They have nothing in them novel or distinctive. I say, "All these things I have known from my youth up."

What attracts me is the brave and sweeping negations directed against all ecclesiastical claims to supremacy over the individual intellect. I belong to the Unitarian Church because its bond of fellowship is sufficient for me: "In the love of Truth and in the spirit of Jesus, we unite for the worship of God and the service of man." If any one says, That is not the definition of a sect, but a wide statement of the purpose of the Holy Catholic Church, I heartily agree with him, for it is

the Holy Catholic Church that I want to belong to.

I am a wayfaring man seeking a well organized and triumphant church "lofty as the
love of God and ample as the wants of man."
I have not found it yet, and I do not identify
it with any existing sect. The church which
I long for will be the organization of the religious life in a more inclusive way. Men of
all denominations are seeking it. I have
joined with the people called Unitarians because while they cherish the ideals of universal religion they do not ask me to pledge
formal allegiance to something bad.

THE SALT OF NORDIC AMERICA

EMINENT AMERICANS

Percentage of Sons of the following who achieve
eminence:

Skilled Laborers	.06
Farmers	.15
Business Men	1.25
Professional Men	2.
Methodist Clergymen	1.
Baptist Clergymen	2.3
Presbyterian Clergymen	9.
Episcopalian Clergymen	11.7
Unitarian Clergymen	15.

TWELVE MODERN APOSTLES

Unity vs. Trinity
Related to Fourth Century Arianism
Organized in Transylvania in 1568
King's Chapel, Boston, First in U. S.
American Unitarian Association organized in Boston in
    1825.
Now 425 Churches in U. S.
Some outstanding Unitarians:

John Adams, William Cullen Bryant, Ralph Waldo
    Emerson, Benjamin Franklin, Oliver Wendell Holmes,
    Henry Wadsworth Longfellow, Daniel Webster, Presi-
    dent Taft.

CHAPTER X

WHY I AM A MORMON

By

REED SMOOT

United States Senator From Utah

IN the first place, I was born one. My parents were among the early converts to the teachings of Joseph Smith, the founder of the Church of Jesus Christ of Latter-day Saints—my father in Kentucky, his native state; my mother in far-off Norway. What is commonly known as "Mormonism" had no stauncher adherents than Abraham Owen Smoot and his wife, Anna Kerstina Morrison. That I should have imbibed, from infancy, in the home that sheltered them, the spirit of the religion for which either of them would have laid down life, if necessary, will occasion no surprise to the readers of this article. I was the third-born in the household, and Salt Lake City was my birth-place. Since ten years of

[175]

age, however, I have resided in the town of Provo, fifty miles south of the Utah capital.

What education I received as a youth was in "Mormon" schools, notably the Brigham Young Academy at Provo, an institution that my father helped to found. I was one of twenty-nine students with which, in the autumn of 1876, it began its first term. I was then in my fifteenth year.

The founding of the Brigham Young Academy (now University), the parent of a flourishing school system entirely distinct from the public schools, and maintained by the Latter-day Saints at an annual cost of three-quarters of a million dollars, was the outgrowth of a sentiment which demanded spiritual as well as mental and physical education for the children of the "Mormon" community. Joseph Smith was the author of such sayings as these:

"The glory of God is intelligence."

"It is impossible to be saved in ignorance."

"Seek learning by study and also by faith."

"Whatever principles of intelligence we attain to in this life will rise with us in the resurrection; and any man who, by his greater diligence acquires more knowledge than another, will have just that much advantage in the world to come."

The Prophet was true to his principles. He established schools and championed the cause of education. A "Mormon" writer has said: "His educational ideals passed over the threshold of Time and strode down the halls of eternity. With a full appreciation of the knowledge that makes men and women capable and skillful in this life, he prized and taught others to prize, above all, the knowledge that maketh wise unto salvation. How to make a living here—how to solve life's everyday problems, was, of course, important; but how to grapple successfully with the mightier problems of the Great Hereafter,—how to store up treasures in heaven and lay hold upon eternal life, was far more consequential. Education meant to him the leading out of all the latent potential powers of the individual,—the training to perfection of every divine attribute in man, as the child of God and as a god himself, in embryo. He stood for the full and complete development of the soul, body and spirit combined,—mental, physical, moral, and spiritual education, —the education contemplated and inculcated by the Gospel of Jesus Christ."

In the Brigham Young Academy were

taught, along with the ordinary branches of learning, the doctrines of Christ's Gospel. The Bible, the Book of Mormon, and other church publications were among the text books of the institution. Prayer and testimony were required of the students, and the atmosphere of worship pervaded the class rooms. The result was that graduates from this school went forth from its portals firm in the faith, believers in God and in the principles of salvation, equipped not only for expert office work, and skilled labor of various kinds, but also for intelligent and efficient service in the Church schools and mission fields. Being a graduate myself, I shared in the advantages of such a training; and this, without doubt, is one reason why I am a "Mormon." Incidentally I will remark that Utah, which is still overwhelmingly "Mormon" in population, ranks among the leading States of the Union, educationally.

But birth and early training are not the only causes of one's conversion, if it be real and genuine. In my intercourse with the world I have had ample opportunity to come in contact with other religious systems and to compare them with my own. If "Mormonism" is my preference over all, it is because it appeals to me as the most reasonable of all, the most soul-satisfying religion that I have encountered anywhere.

It teaches that man is literally the child of God, fashioned in His image, endowed with divine attributes, and capable, by education and development, of becoming like unto that glorious Being, in whose image or likeness all men are created.

It teaches that this earth, which is but one of millions like it, formed for similar purposes, was made, not out of nothing, as some theologians assert, but out of the eternal elements, spirit and matter, and that after it has filled the measure of its creation as a temporary abode, a place of probation for man, it will be converted into a celestial sphere, that the righteous may inherit it forever. Christ's millennial reign is to sanctify the earth and prepare it for celestial glory.

"Mormonism" teaches that the glorified planets are God's kingdoms, and that to each kingdom a law is given. Whosoever inherits any one of these kingdoms,—celestial, terrestrial, or telestial,—must abide the law pertaining to that kingdom; all heavenly gifts, whether spiritual or temporal, being predicated upon the principle of obedience.

The Gospel plan, instituted by the Great Creator in the beginning, was designed for the promotion of the lesser intelligences in the midst of which He found himself, the most intelligent of all. This plan includes man's fall and redemption, both of which were divinely preordained, and are steps in the march of eternal progression. The condition of this promotion,—this advancement of the preexistent intelligences who become mortal men and women, is their obedience to the principles of the Gospel. They must have faith, must repent of their sins, must be baptized for the remission of sins, must receive the Holy Ghost by the laying on of hands, and do all else that the Lord requires of them.

They who "kept the first estate,"—like in the spirit world,—are given a second estate,—life on earth, where they demonstrate their worthiness or unworthiness of eternal glory. Satan and his legions, one-third of Heaven's spirit host, kept not their first estate, and because of their rebellion were not permitted to take bodies, which are a means of eternal increase and exaltation; but two-thirds of that great family of spirits, for their faithfulness in the previous life, were or will yet be given fleshly tabernacles, thus becoming "living souls," with opportunities for education in the midst of life's vicissitudes.

All men are to be rewarded according to their works, as shown to John the Revelator in his great vision on Patmos. They who inherit celestial glory, the highest heavenly condition, which is comparable to the light of the sun, are they who receive the gospel in this life; also those who would receive it if the opportunity were offered. They can believe and repent in the spirit world, and receive baptism by proxy in temples erected on earth for that purpose. These are the valiant, who obey Christ in all things.

The inheritors of terrestrial glory are they who yield a partial, but not a full obedience to the divine commands. They receive not the gospel here, but afterwards receive it, and their glory is likened unto that of the moon. Telestial glory is for those who are cast down to hell, are there purged of their sins, and after paying their debt to Eternal Justice, are released from prison, to receive that for which they are fitted and prepared. They are as the twinkling stars, and are servants of the Most High, "but where God and Christ dwell they cannot come, worlds without end."

All men will be saved except the sons of perdition, who have had every opportunity, not only for salvation, but for exaltation to the highest glory; and then have denied, trampled upon and thrown it all away. These are the only ones who cannot be saved in some degree of glory; and the reason why they are lost, is because they have sinned away the power of repentance, upon which all salvation is predicated.

These doctrines look reasonable to me. They are scriptural and consistent. They appeal to my sense of justice, of mercy, and of right. They measure up to the eternal fitness of things. I have never found anything better in my researches for spiritual light, and because of this and my conviction that they are true, I am a "Mormon."

My religion proclaims itself to be the Everlasting Gospel, framed in the heavens before this earth was formed, and revealed to man in a series of dispensations, of which the present one,—the dispensation of the fullness of times,—is the greatest and the last. The

Gospel's restoration in this age is preliminary to the gathering of the scattered house of Israel; Zion in America and Jerusalem in Palestine being the places where they will assemble to meet their God and King, who is coming to reign literally upon the earth. The Gentiles, with their wealth and power, their steamships, railroads, and other means of rapid transit and communication, are taking part in this work, and will share in the benefits that flow from it. This age is destined to witness the consummation of God's purposes in relation to this planet.

The movement known as "Mormonism" was made possible, humanly speaking, by the establishment of the government of the United States, whose constitutional guarantee of religious liberty paved the way for the coming forth of this "marvelous work and wonder." Such is the "Mormon" position.

The Latter-day Saints believe that they must be loyal to their country, honoring its laws, upholding its institutions, its constituted authorities, and doing all things that American citizens ought to do. They are taught that the Constitution of the United States was inspired of God and framed by wise men whom the Almighty raised up for this very purpose, and that it "should be maintained for the rights and protection of all flesh," so that every man may act according to the moral agency which God has given him, that he "may be accountable for his own sins in the day of judgment."

Believing this, they cannot be otherwise than loyal. They do not blame the government of the United States for their past persecutions at the hands of lawless mobs. They realize that such things were not because of the Constitution and the Government, but in spite of them; and they stand ready at all times to honor the laws of this nation and to defend it against foes without or within. It is because I know this that I am a "Mormon."

Indoctrinated from childhood in the principles of the Church to which I belong, I give my hearty adherence to its Articles of Faith, as penned and published by Joseph Smith, the Prophet. They are as follows:

1. We believe in God, the Eternal Father, and in His Son, Jesus Christ, and in the Holy Ghost.

2. We believe that men will be punished for their own sins, and not for Adam's transgression.

3. We believe that through the Atonement of Christ,

all mankind may be saved, by obedience to the laws and ordinances of the Gospel.

4. We believe that the first principles and ordinances of the Gospel are: first, Faith in the Lord Jesus Christ; second, Repentance; third, Baptism by immersion for the remission of sins; fourth, Laying on of hands for the gift of the Holy Ghost.

5. We believe that a man must be called of God, by prophecy, and by the laying on of hands, by those who are in authority, to preach the Gospel and administer in the ordinances thereof.

6. We believe in the same organization that existed in the Primitive Church, viz., apostles, prophets, pastors, teachers, evangelists, etc.

7. We believe in the gift of tongues, prophecy, revelation, visions, healing, interpretation of tongues, etc.

8. We believe the Bible to be the word of God as far as it is translated correctly; we also believe the Book of Mormon to be the word of God.

9. We believe all that God has revealed, all that He does now reveal, and we believe that He will yet reveal many great and important things pertaining to the Kingdom of God.

10. We believe in the literal gathering of Israel and in the restoration of the Ten Tribes; that Zion will be built upon this (the American) continent; that Christ will reign personally upon the earth; and that the earth will be renewed and receive its paradisiacal glory.

11. We claim the privilege of worshiping Almighty God according to the dictates of our own conscience, and

allow all men the same privilege, let them worship how, where, or what they may.

12. We believe in being subject to kings, presidents, rulers, and magistrates, in obeying, honoring, and sustaining the law.

13. We believe in being honest, true, chaste, benevolent, virtuous, and in doing good to all men; indeed, we may say that we follow the admonition of Paul—We believe all things, we hope all things, we have endured many things, and hope to be able to endure all things. If there is anything virtuous, lovely, or of good report or praiseworthy, we seek after these things.

In conclusion, I am a "Mormon" because I have received a convincing testimony that Joseph Smith's mission was of God; that he lived to do good and died a martyr; and that his successors, in building upon the foundation that he laid, have been and are carrying out the will of God, with the welfare of all men in view.

CHURCH OF JESUS CHRIST OF LATTER-DAY SAINTS

MEMBERS

Utah	*300,000*
Idaho	*85,000*
Arizona	*12,000*

Colorado	4,000
Scattered U. S.	120,000
Hawaii	12,500
Europe	37,000
Other Countries	29,500
Total Mormons	600,000

MORMON MILESTONES

December 23, 1805—Joseph Smith born in Sharon, Vermont.

April, 1820—He beheld the Father and the Son.

September 21, 1823—The Angel Moroni revealed to him the plates of the Book of Mormon on Cumorah Hill near Manchester, Ontario County, N. Y.

1828-1830—Translated the Book of Mormon.

April 6, 1830—The Church organized at Fayette, Seneca County, N. Y.

December 25, 1832—Joseph Smith prophesied the Civil War and the World War.

1831-1844—Headquarters moved to Ohio, to Missouri, to Illinois.

June 27, 1844—Joseph Smith and his brother, Hyrum, killed by mob at Carthage, Illinois.

1844—Brigham Young succeeded as presiding officer.

1846—Church expelled from Illinois.

July 24, 1847—The pioneers entered Salt Lake Valley, Utah, under Brigham Young.

TWELVE MODERN APOSTLES

August 29, 1877—Brigham Young, "Empire Builder,"
died.
1882—Congress passed Edmunds Law forbidding poly-
gamy in U. S. territories.
1896—Utah admitted as a state to the Union

CHAPTER XI

WHY I AM A CHRISTIAN
SCIENTIST

By

CLIFFORD SMITH
Chairman of Publication Committee

PROBABLY the words Christian Science
were used first by the Reverend Dr. William Adams, a clergyman of the Episcopal
Church. He wrote a book entitled *"The Elements of Christian Science*, a Treatise upon
Moral Philosophy and Practice," which was
published in 1850. The latter part of this
title indicates the contents of the book.

The religion she named Christian Science
was discovered by Mary Baker Eddy in 1866.
She chose this term as the proper name for
what she also described as "the scientific system of divine healing" (*Science and Health
with Key to the Scriptures,* p. 123). As
formulated by Mrs. Eddy, Christian Science
is a system of religious teaching and practise

[189]

based on what it presents as the absolute truth of being. For this truth, it depends chiefly on the words and the works of Christ Jesus. "The Bible has been my only authority" (Idem, p. 1263).

After appropriate preparation, Mrs. Eddy prepared a comprehensive statement of her teaching (the book just mentioned) which was published in 1875. At intervals from then until near the end of her human life, she revised this book, doing so "only to give a clearer and fuller expression of its original meaning" (Idem, p. 361). It has been given to nearly all public libraries where English is spoken, has been translated into French and German, and has had an enormous sale. Over two thousand Christian Science reading rooms are maintained by the churches of this denomination, largely for the convenience of all who may wish to borrow or study this book.

The Christian Science denomination was founded in 1876. At first it consisted of Mrs. Eddy and six of her students. Reorganized in 1879, and again in 1892, it consists at present of The Mother Church, The First Church of Christ, Scientist, in Boston, two thousand and two hundred and fifty branches of this Church, which are known as Churches of Christ, Scientist, or Christian Science Societies, and individual Christian Scientists at as many or more other places where there are not yet enough adherents for formal organizations. In short, the Christian Science denomination or Church of Christ, Scientist, has already had a very remarkable growth; and it is composed of people who are notable for their devotion, their intelligence, and their good deeds.

My first step toward Christian Science was taken without any thought of this religion. It was taken by endeavoring to read the New Testament as if it presented a subject which was new to me. That is to say, I endeavored to read this authentic record of original Christianity without being influenced by my previous acceptance of Christianity as it was commonly taught thirty years ago. By doing this, I concluded that many of the creedal and doctrinal statements of that time were not based upon and were not consistent with the recorded saying of Christ Jesus. In particular, I concluded that the Christian teaching with which I was familiar did not attribute enough importance to what was said by Christ

Jesus himself as to the method and purpose of his ministry. For instance, I allude to such sayings as "To this end was I born, and for this cause came I into the world, that I should bear witness unto the truth" (John 18:37).

Originally the religion taught and practised by Christ Jesus was called the way, the new and living way, the way of the truth, while he was regarded as the one who showed this way. The first of these facts is attested by Acts 9:2, 19:23, 22:4, 24:22; Hebrews 10:20; II Peter 2:2, and other passages in the New Testament, while the second is attested by John 14:16, 18:37; Hebrews 10:20, and other citations. The New Testament also shows that the Christian religion was based originally on the truth of being, the absolute or spiritual truth concerning God and man. (See Matthew 15:13, 23:9; John 3:4-8, 6:63, 8:32, 18:37, and other citations.) So I became interested in Christian Science because its theology appealed to me as being identical with that of the Four Gospels, and because I found afterward by personal experience that its practise is effective for the purpose of healing in the broadest sense of this term. Subsequent experience and observation have given me the abiding conviction that this teaching and practise is fulfilling and is destined completely to fulfil the promise of original Christianity.

Christian Science begins by regarding God as the cause, the origin, the divine Principle of all that really is. To define God further, it employs frequently the word Good, besides such terms as Life, Love, Truth, and such terms as Mind, Soul, Spirit. This religion also regards God as the infinite Person, and as being one, not three. The attitude of this teaching toward all forms of evil is shown by the following quotation from the Christian Science textbook: "All reality is in God and His creation, harmonious and eternal. That which He creates is good, and He makes all that is made. Therefore the only reality of sin, sickness, or death is the awful fact that unrealities seem real to human, erring belief, until God strips off their disguise. They are not true, because they are not of God" (*Science and Health,* p. 472).

The most distinctive features of Christian Science are its practise and the results from its practise. This religion maintains that the truth of being,—the truth concerning God and man,—includes a rule for its practise and a law by which it produces effects. To a certain extent, Jesus declared this rule and law when he said, "Ye shall know the truth, and the truth shall make you free" (John 8:32). Accordingly, for the individual Christian to gain his freedom from any form of error, he should know the truth, the absolute truth of being, applicable to his case; and Christian Science teaches that the truth of being is effective when used by one individual for another, because such is the unity of real being and such is the law of God. For this reason, evidently, Jesus could and did declare the possibility of Christian healing in unlimited terms. (See Matthew 10:5-10; 26:16-20; Mark 16:14-18; John 14:12.)

The practise of Christian Science is not merely mental; it must be also spiritual. The nonspiritual elements in the so-called human mind do not contribute to harmony or health. The practitioner must know or realize spiritually, and his ability to do this is derived from the divine Mind. Therefore, he must agree with the Teacher and Way-shower, who said, "I can of mine own self do nothing," (John 5:30), and must prepare for the healing ministry and keep in condition for it by living the life of a genuine Christian.

Christian Science healing has been practised successfully since 1867. Mrs. Eddy having been healed from the effects of a severe injury at the time of her discovery in 1866, she began within a year to demonstrate her newly found understanding of truth by healing other sufferers. Now, the efficacy of Christian Science practise is attested by a great multitude of witnesses, some of whom are to be found in nearly every part of the world. The practise of Christian Science is not limited, as is commonly supposed, to functional disorders; nor is this practise limited, as is also commonly supposed, to the healing of the sick. On the contrary, Christian Scientists regard their religion as being applicable practically to every human need.

Christian Science, therefore, is a way of living that finds its chief inspiration, its perfect illustration, and its complete proof in the life of Christ Jesus. It reveals, awakens, and develops the possibilities that exist, latently, in everyone. It teaches how to throw off the inabilities, the disabilities, and the liabilities that have been imposed on men by ages of

erroneous thinking, and how to gain true man-
hood. It destroys and prevents disease by lift-
ing thought above the cause and condition of
the disorder into the Kingdom of God,—into
the atmosphere of divine Life, Love, and
Truth. It explains miracles of healing and
reformation as acts of power done in accordance with divine law. It advances the reform
of social conditions by defining the obligations
of the individual to God and to fellow-men
in practical terms of service. It proves that
heaven is not merely the future home or state
of the righteous, but is the present result of
being and doing good, of right thinking and
right doing. Since it is compassionate, helpful, and spiritual, it is Christian. Since it is
methodical and calls for exact knowledge and
is based on divine Principle, it is Science. In
short, Christian Science meets human needs,
and it does this in the way that promises in
due course completely to deliver humanity
from the bondage of error or evil. These are
the reasons why I am a Christian Scientist.

CORNERSTONES IN CHRISTIAN SCIENCE

Christian Science discovered by Mary Baker Eddy 1866
"Science and Health" published *1875*
Denomination founded *1876*
Church organized *1879*
Reorganized with Mother Church in Boston *1892*
Passing on of Mary Baker Eddy *1910*
1500 churches and societies throughout the world in 1915
2253 churches and societies throughout the world in 1926

DISTRIBUTION

United States	*1930*
Canada	*56*
British Isles	*164*
France	*2*
Germany	*30*
Switzerland	*11*
Austria	*1*
Italy	*2*
Holland	*4*
Russia	*1*
Latvia	*1*
Scandinavian Countries	*5*
Central and South America	*7*
South Africa	*13*
Australasia	*19*
Far East	*7*

CHAPTER XII

WHY I AM AN UNBELIEVER

By

CARL VAN DOREN

LET us be honest. There have always been men and women without the gift of faith. They lack it, do not desire it, and would not know what to do with it if they had it. They are apparently no less intelligent than the faithful, and apparently no less virtuous. How great the number of them is it would be difficult to say, but they exist in all communities and are most numerous where there is most enlightenment. As they have no organization and no creed, they can of course have no official spokesman. Nevertheless, any one of them who speaks out can be trusted to speak, in a way, for all of them. Like the mystics, the unbelievers, wherever found, are essentially of one spirit and one language. I cannot, however, pretend to represent more than a single complexion of unbelief.

The very terms which I am forced to use put me at the outset in a trying position. Belief, being first in the field, naturally took a positive term for itself and gave a negative term to unbelief. As an unbeliever, I am therefore obliged to seem merely to dissent from the believers, no matter how much more I may do. Actually I do more. What they call unbelief, I call belief. Doubtless I was born to it, but I have tested it with reading and speculation, and I hold it firmly. What I have referred to as the gift of faith I do not, to be exact, regard as a gift. I regard it, rather, as a survival from an earlier stage of thinking and feeling: in short, as a form of superstition. It, and not the thing I am forced to name unbelief, seems to me negative. It denies the reason. It denies the evidences in the case, in the sense that it insists upon introducing elements which come not from the facts as shown but from the imaginations and wishes of mortals. Unbelief does not deny the reason and it sticks as closely as it can to the evidences.

I shall have to be more explicit. When I

say I am an unbeliever, I do not mean merely
that I am no Mormon or no Methodist, or
even that I am no Christian or no Buddhist.
These seem to me relatively unimportant divisions and subdivisions of belief. I mean
that I do not believe in any god that has ever
been devised, in any doctrine that has ever
claimed to be revealed, in any scheme of immortality that has ever been expounded.

As to gods, they have been, I find, countless,
but even the names of most of them lie in the
deep compost which is known as civilization,
and the memories of few of them are green.
There does not seem to me to be good reason
for holding that some of them are false and
some of them, or one of them, true. Each was
created by the imaginations and wishes of men
who could not account for the behavior of the
universe in any other satisfactory way. But
no god has satisfied his worshipers forever.
Sooner or later they have realized that the
attributes once ascribed to him, such as
selfishness or lustfulness or vengefulness, are
unworthy of the moral systems which men
have evolved among themselves. Thereupon
follows the gradual doom of the god, however
long certain of the faithful may cling to his

cult. In the case of the god who still survives
in the loyalty of men after centuries of scrutiny, it can always be noted that little besides
his name has endured. His attributes will
have been so revised that he is really another
god. Nor is this objection met by the argument that the concept of the god has been
purified while the essence of him survived.
In the concept alone can he be studied; the
essence eludes the grasp of the human mind.
I may prefer among the various gods that god
who seems to me most thoroughly purged of
what I regard as undivine elements, but I
make my choice, obviously, upon principles
which come from observation of the conduct
of men. Whether a god has been created in
the image of gross desires or of pure desires
does not greatly matter. The difference proves
merely that different men have desired gods
and have furnished themselves with the gods
they were able to conceive. Behind all their
conceptions still lies the abyss of ignorance.
There is no trustworthy evidence as to a god's
absolute existence.

Nor does the thing called revelation, as I
see it, carry the proof further. All the
prophets swear that a god speaks through

them, and yet they prophesy contradictions. Once more, men must choose in accordance with their own principles. That a revelation was announced long ago makes it difficult to examine, but does not otherwise attest its soundness. That some revealed doctrine has lasted for ages and has met the needs of many generations proves that it is the kind of doctrine which endures and satisfies, but not that it is divine. Secular doctrines which turned out to be perfectly false have also endured and satisfied. If belief in a god has to proceed from the assumption that he exists, belief in revelation has first to proceed from the assumption that a god exists and then to go further to the assumption that he communicates his will to certain men. But both are mere assumptions. Neither is, in the present state of knowledge, at all capable of proof. Suppose a god did exist, and suppose he did communicate his will to any of his creatures. What man among them could comprehend that language? What man could take that dictation? And what man could overwhelmingly persuade his fellows that he had been selected and that they must accept him as authentic? The best they could do would be to have faith in two assumptions and to test the revealed will by its correspondence to their imaginations and wishes. At this point it may be contended that revelation must be real because it arouses so much response in so many human bosoms. This does not follow without a leap of the reason into the realm of hypothesis. Nothing is proved by this general response except that men are everywhere very much alike. They have the same members, the same organs, the same glands, in varying degrees of activity. Being so much alike, they tend to agree upon a few primary desires. Fortunate the religion by which those desires appear to be gratified.

One desire by which the human mind is often teased is the desire to live after death. It is not difficult to explain. Men live so briefly that their plans far outrun their ability to execute them. They see themselves cut off before their will to live is exhausted. Naturally enough, they wish to survive, and, being men, believe in their chances for survival. But their wishes afford no possible proof. Life covers the earth with wishes, as it covers the earth with plants and animals. No wish, however, is evidence of anything beyond itself. Let millions hold it, and it is still only a wish. Let each separate race exhibit it, and it is still only a wish. Let the wisest hold it as strongly as the foolishest, and it is still only a wish. Whoever says he knows that immortality is a fact is merely hoping that it is. And whoever argues, as men often do, that life would be meaningless without immortality, because it alone brings justice into human fate, must first argue, as no man has ever quite convincingly done, that life has an unmistakable meaning and that it is just. I, at least, am convinced on neither of these two points. Though I am, I believe, familiar with all the arguments, I do not find any of them notably better than the others. All I see is that the wish for immortality is wide-spread, that certain schemes of immortality imagined from it have here or there proved more agreeable than rival schemes, and that they have been more generally accepted. The religions which provide these successful schemes I can credit with keener insight into human wishes than other religions have had, but I cannot credit them with greater authority as regards the truth. They are all guesswork.

That I think thus about gods, revelation,

and immortality ought to be sufficient answer to the question why I am an unbeliever. It would be if the question were always reasonably asked, but it is not. There is also an emotional aspect to be considered. Many believers, I am told, have the same doubts, and yet have the knack of putting their doubts to sleep and entering ardently into the communion of the faithful. The process is incomprehensible to me. So far as I understand it, such believers are moved by their desires to the extent of letting them rule not only their conduct but their thoughts. An unbeliever's desires have, apparently, less power over his reason. Perhaps this is only another way of saying that his strongest desire is to be as reasonable as he can. However the condition be interpreted, the consequence is the same. An honest unbeliever can no more make himself believe against his reason than he can make himself free of the pull of gravitation. For myself, I feel no obligation whatever to believe. I might once have felt it prudent to keep silence, for I perceive that the race of men, while sheep in credulity, are wolves for conformity; but just now, happily, in this breathing-spell of toleration, there are so

many varieties of belief that even an unbeliever may speak out.

In so doing, I must answer certain secondary questions which unbelievers are often
asked. Does it not persuade me, one question
runs, to realize that many learned men have
pondered upon supernatural matters and have
been won over to belief? I answer, not in the
least. With respect to the gods, revelation,
and immortality no man is enough more
learned than his fellows to have the right to
insist that they follow him into the regions
about which all men are ignorant. I am not
a particle more impressed by some good old
man's conviction that he is in the confidence
of the gods than I am by any boy's conviction
that there are fish in the horse-pond from
which no fish has ever been taken. Does it
not impress me to see some good old woman
serene in the faith of a blessed immortality?
No more than it impresses me to see a little
girl full of trust in the universal munificence
of a Christmas saint. Am I not moved by the
spectacle of a great tradition of worship which
has broadened out over continents and which
brings all its worshipers punctually together
in the observance of noble and dignified rites?

Yes, but I am moved precisely by that as I am moved by the specacle of men everywhere putting their seed seasonably in the ground, tending its increase, and patiently gathering in their harvests.

Finally, do I never suspect in myself some moral obliquity, or do I not at least regret the bleak outlook of unbelief? On these points I am, in my own mind, as secure as I know how to be. There is no moral obligation to believe what is unbelievable, any more than there is a moral obligation to do what is undoable. Even in religion, honesty is a virtue. Obliquity, I should say, shows itself rather in prudent pretense or in voluntary self-delusion. Furthermore, the unbelievers have, as I read history, done less harm to the world than the believers. They have not filled it with savage wars or snarled casuistries, with crusades or persecutions, with complacency or ignorance. They have, instead, done what they could to fill it with knowledge and beauty, with temperance and justice, with manners and laughter. They have numbered among themselves some of the most distinguished specimens of mankind. And when they have been undistinguished, they have surely not been inferior to the believers in the fine art of minding their own affairs and so of enlarging the territories of peace.

Nor is the outlook of unbelief, to my way of thinking, a bleak one. It is merely rooted in courage and not in fear. Belief is still in the plight of those ancient races who out of a lack of knowledge peopled the forest with satyrs and the sea with ominous monsters and the ends of the earth with misshapen anthropophagi. So the pessimists among believers have peopled the void with witches and devils, and the optimists among them have peopled it with angels and gods. Both alike have been afraid to furnish the house of life simply. They have cluttered it with the furniture of faith. Much of this furniture, the most reasonable unbeliever would never think of denying, is very beautiful. There are breathing myths, there are comforting legends, there are consoling hopes. But they have, as the unbeliever sees them, no authority beyond that of poetry. That is, they may captivate if they can, but they have no right to insist upon conquering. Beliefs, like tastes, may differ. The unbeliever's taste and belief are austere. In the wilderness of worlds he does not yield to the temptation to belittle the others by magnifying his own. Among the dangers of chance he does not look for safety to any watchful providence whose special concern he imagines he is. Though he knows that knowledge is imperfect, he trusts it alone. If he takes, therefore, the less delight in metaphysics, he takes the more in physics. Each discovery of a new truth brings him a vivid joy. He builds himself up, so far as he can, upon truth, and barricades himself with it. Thus doing, he never sags into superstition, but grows steadily more robust and blithe in his courage. However many fears he may prove unable to escape, he does not multiply them in his imagination and then combat them with his wishes. Austerity may be simplicity and not bleakness.

Does the unbeliever lack certain of the gentler virtues of the believer, the quiet confidence, the unquestioning obedience? He may, yet it must always be remembered that the greatest believers are the greatest tyrants. If the freedom rather than the tyranny of faith is to better the world, then the betterment lies in the hands, I think, of the unbelievers. At any rate, I take my stand with them.